William Joynson Cocker

Hand-book of punctuation, with instructions for capitalization, letter-writing, and proof-reading

William Joynson Cocker

Hand-book of punctuation, with instructions for capitalization, letter-writing, and proof-reading

ISBN/EAN: 9783337229443

Printed in Europe, USA, Canada, Australia, Japan

Cover: Foto ©Lupo / pixelio.de

More available books at **www.hansebooks.com**

HAND-BOOK

OF

PUNCTUATION,

WITH INSTRUCTIONS FOR

CAPITALIZATION, LETTER-WRITING,
AND
PROOF-READING,

BY

W. J. COCKER, A. M.

A. S. BARNES & CO.,
NEW YORK, CHICAGO, AND NEW ORLEANS.
1878.

PREFACE.

As the pronunciation of words is determined by the usage of the best speakers, so, in a great measure, the punctuation of sentences is based on the usage of the best writers. Recognizing this fact, the author has aimed,—

1. To state such general rules as are recognized by most writers of good English.

2. To illustrate these rules by examples taken from many of our best English classics.

3. To give some of the differences in usage that exist even among the best of writers.

It is frequently asserted that even good writers differ so much in their use of punctuation marks that it is impossible to lay down any general rules, and that it is better for each one to consult his own taste and judgment. With equal reason it might be said that inasmuch as good speakers, and even lexicographers, differ in the pronunciation of words, therefore each speaker should make his own taste and judgment the standard for correct pronunciation. A writer's mode of expressing his thoughts will determine the character and number of the punctuation marks that he uses, and it is chiefly owing to this that even good writers differ somewhat in punctuating what they have written. There are some rules that are invariable under all circumstances; the use of others depends on the mental characteristics of the writer; and there are still other rules, the application of which is determined by the writer's taste alone.

By gestures, tones of voice, oratorical pauses, emphasis, and in various ways, a speaker can make his meaning clear to his listeners; and so a writer should certainly use all the aids which punctuation, capitals, and italics afford, in presenting clearly what he has written for the perusal of others. Business men, however, seem to think that they are not amenable to the rules that govern good writers. They affirm that they have no time to punctuate their letters, and yet they subject others to the necessity of expending time and patience in trying to make out their meaning. Serious misunderstandings have arisen between business men, in consequence of the omission or incorrect use of punctuation marks, and expensive lawsuits have originated in the careless punctuation of legal instruments.

Very little attention is paid in our public schools to punctuation, and the rules usually given in English Composition are either disregarded or not properly understood. This may, perhaps, be accounted for by the fact that the rules are wanting in clearness, and are not sufficiently illustrated by examples. The aim of this volume is to remedy, in some measure, these evils, and to secure more attention to what ought to be a prominent part of school instruction. The evils of bad punctuation are really more serious than the evils of bad spelling, and no student can be said to have learned to read well, much less to write well, who has not studied punctuation intelligently.

We would suggest that this hand-book be used at Rhetorical Exercises, and that when essays, orations, criticisms, &c., are handed to the teacher for correction, he should use a red or a blue pencil, so that corrections may be the more readily recognized. Besides the corrections in grammar, spelling, &c., he should be careful to supply punctuation marks when needed, cross out needless ones, and, of course, make such other corrections as may be necessary. When the productions are returned to the pupils, the teacher should first point out the necessity of using certain marks, in order to define and bring out the meaning, and to show the relation between the different members of a sentence. Having thus shown the need of punctuation marks, then reference should be made to some of the simpler rules, to impress this need on the mind. Great care should be taken not to perplex the mind with too many rules before the necessity is created for their use. The great difficulty in the study of punctuation has been that many rules are committed to memory before the need of their use has arisen, so that the mind is perplexed and bewildered instead of enlightened. The rule, it must be remembered, does not create the necessity; the necessity creates the rule. Then, again, we think a great mistake is made by having the beginner punctuate what some one else has written. The better plan is for the pupil, at the very outset, to punctuate what he himself has composed, and in his effort to bring out his own meaning clearly, he will, with the aid of a few rules, almost intuitively fall into the habit of punctuating correctly.

The following suggestions may be of service:—

1. Do not give a pupil a rule to learn, unless it is clearly founded upon examples taken from what he himself has written.

2. Take, at first, the simplest, most frequently used, and most readily understood rules.

3. Advance slowly, remembering that a few simple principles clearly understood, are of much more practical benefit than a number of misty rules hastily committed to memory.

In the preparation of this hand-book, the author is under obligations to various authorities, but he is more especially indebted to Wilson's "Treatise on Punctuation."

W. J. COCKER.

ADRIAN, Mich., Dec. 26, 1877.

Table of Contents.

I. Punctuation .... pp. 1– 53
II. Capitals 54– 70
III. Letter-Forms .... " 71–100
IV. Proof-Reading .... " 101–114
V. Index .... ' 115–127

Introduction.

The principal punctuation marks are,—
1. The Comma ,
2. The Semicolon ;
3. The Colon :
4. The Period .

The comma indicates a somewhat close relationship between the parts of a sentence; the semicolon, a more distant relationship; the colon indicates that the parts are almost independent of each other; the period marks the close of a sentence, and indicates that a thought is complete.

In simple sentences, when the words are closely united together, and the relationship of the words to each other is readily perceived, there is usually no need of any punctuation marks, except a period at the close. It should always be borne in mind that punctuation marks are used primarily to assist in bringing out the meaning of the writer, and not to embellish a written or a printed page. In sentences made up of parts that are closely related to each other, but, at the same time, distinct in character, commas should be used. They are way-marks for the accommodation of the reader. A production unpunctuated presents as dreary a prospect to the reader, as the level plain of Chaldæa presents to the perplexed traveler who has lost himself among the sandy mounds on the banks of the Euphrates, and has nothing by which to direct his course.

When the different parts of a sentence are somewhat disconnected, and not closely related to each other, a semicolon or colon should be used. Sentences are sometimes very long and complicated. It is then necessary to separate the main divisions by semicolons, and the smaller by commas. Sometimes the smaller parts of a sentence are separated by commas and semicolons, and the main divisions by colons.

The other marks in use are,—

1. The Interrogation Point ?
2. The Exclamation Point !
3. The Dash —
4. Marks of Parenthesis ( )
5. Brackets [ ]
6. Quotation Marks " ' ' "
7. The Apostrophe '
8. The Hyphen -
9. Miscellaneous marks.

THE COMMA.

INTRODUCTORY REMARKS.

In order to properly understand some of the rules that are given in the following pages, it is absolutely necessary to have a clear understanding of the difference between a sentence and a clause. A sentence is a combination of words expressing a complete thought, and usually followed by a period; a clause is a distinct part of a sentence. Some sentences are simple in form, and have but one subject and one finite verb; as, "Language is part of a man's character."—*Coleridge.* Other sentences are made up of clauses, each clause having a subject and a verb; in other words, several clauses are sometimes joined together to form one sentence; as, "New forms of beauty start at once into existence, and all the burial places of the memory give up their dead."—*Macaulay.* It will be easily seen that clauses will be more readily recognized with the eye, and more easily comprehended, if they are separated from each other by punctuation marks. This will be especially so, if the clauses are long.

In preparing this hand-book, the aim has been to avoid, as much as possible, the use of technical terms. Whenever such terms are used, explanations will usually be found under the head of *Remarks.*

Rule I. *Independent Clauses.*—Independent clauses should be separated from each other by commas.

EXAMPLES.

"Savage was discomposed by the intrusion or omission of a comma, and he would lament an error of a single letter as a great calamity."—*Dr. Johnson.*

"Man wants but little here below,
Nor wants that little long."—*Goldsmith.*

"Take short views, hope for the best, and trust in God."—*Sydney Smith.*

REMARKS.

1. An independent clause is one that is not dependent on any other clause for the completion of its meaning; as, Take short views | hope for the best | and trust in God. Independent clauses are frequently connected by *and, or, nor, but*.

2. When the clauses are short and closely united, the comma may be omitted; as, "Death had lost its terrors and pleasure its charms."

3. When the clauses are long and divided into smaller portions by commas, they should be separated from each other by semicolons. See Rule I. p. 23.

Rule II. *Dependent Clauses.*—Dependent clauses should be separated from each other by commas.

EXAMPLES.

"If a man does not make new acquaintances as he advances through life, he will soon find himself left alone. A man, Sir, should keep his friendship in constant repair."—*Dr. Johnson.*

"When Dr. Franklin wished to gain his enemy, he asked him to do him a favor."

"Clap an extinguisher upon your irony, if you are unhappily blest with a vein of it."—*Lamb.*

"Although we seldom followed advice, we were all ready enough to ask it."—*Goldsmith.*

REMARKS.

1. A clause is said to be dependent, when it depends on some other clause to complete its meaning; as, When Dr. Johnson wished to gain his enemy | he asked him to do him a favor. The first clause of this sentence would not be complete in meaning without the second. Dependent clauses usually commence with *if*, *when*, *since*, *because*, *until*, &c.

2. When clauses are closely connected, the comma may be omitted; as, Mozart published some music when seven years of age.

RULE III. *Relative Clauses.*—1. A relative clause should be separated from the rest of the sentence by a comma.

2. But the comma should be omitted, when the relative clause is so closely connected with what precedes that it cannot be dropped without destroying the sense.

EXAMPLES.

1. "Men in a corner, who have the unhappiness of conversing too little with present things."—*Swift.*

"The waters are nature's storehouse, in which she locks up her wonders."—*Izaak Walton.*

"He had on a coat made of that cloth called thunder-and-lightning, which, though grown too short, was much too good to be thrown away."—*Goldsmith.*

2. "Althworthy here betook himself to those pleasing slumbers which a heart that hungers after goodness is apt to enjoy when thoroughly satisfied."—*Fielding.*

"A man who is good for making excuses is good for nothing else."—*Dr. Franklin.*

"Like Cæsar, Cortes wrote his own commentaries in the heart of the stirring scenes which form the subject of them."—*Prescott.*

REMARKS.

1. Relative clauses are generally introduced by the relative pronouns *who,* **which,** *that,* or *what.*

2. A comma should be placed before the relative clause, even when it is necessary to complete the meaning of the antecedent,—

   a. When the relative is immediately followed by a word or an expression inclosed in commas; as, "As a man, he may not have deserved the admiration which he received from those, who, bewitched by his fascinating society, worshiped him nightly in his favorite temple at Button's."—*Macaulay.*

b. When the relative has several antecedents that are separated from each other by commas; as, "All those arts, rarities, and inventions, which vulgar minds gaze at, the ingenious pursue, and all admire, are but the relics of an intellect defaced with sin and time."—*South.*

3. The words *of which* are sometimes preceded by a comma, even when they are necessary to complete the meaning of the antecedent: as, "His mind was formed of those firm materials, of which nature formerly hammered out the Stoic, and upon which the sorrows of no man living could make an impression."—*Fielding.*

RULE IV. *Parenthetical Words and Phrases.* When single words and phrases break the connection between closely related parts of a sentence, they should usually be separated by commas from the rest of the sentence.

1. Words used parenthetically,—

therefore,	namely,	however,
indeed,	finally,	moreover,
perhaps,	consequently,	nevertheless, &c.

2. Phrases used parenthetically,—

in short,	in fact,	in reality,
in truth,	in a word,	no doubt,
of course,	you know,	as it were, &c.

EXAMPLES.

1. "As an orator, indeed, he was not magnetic or inspiring".—*G. W. Curtis.*

"There is, perhaps, no surer **mark** of folly, than to **attempt** to correct the natural infirmities of those we love."—*Fielding.*

"There is, however, a limit at which forbearance ceases to be a **virtue.**"—*Burke.*

2. "I had **grown to** my desk, as **it were, and** the wood had **entered my** soul."—***Lamb.***

"In short, he is a memorable instance of what has been **often** observed, that the boy is the man in miniature."—***Boswell.***

REMARKS.

1. **Words** and phrases are said to **be used** parenthetically, when they obstruct, as it were, the **flow of** the **sentence, and** might be dropped without destroying **the sense.**

2. Whenever parenthetical **words and** phrases readily coalesce with the **rest of** the sentence, it is better to omit punctuation marks; **as,** "I am therefore exceedingly unwilling that anything, **however slight,** which my illustrious friend thought it worth while to express, with any degree of point, should perish."—***Boswell.***

3. **A** distinction should **be** made between words used parenthetically, and **adverbs** qualifying particular words; as, "And with learning was united a **mild and** liberal spirit, too often **wanting** in the princely colleges **of Oxford."**—*Macaulay.*

"That, too, has **its eminent service."**—***Burke.***

Rule V. *Parenthetical Expressions.*—Expressions of a parenthetical character should be separated from the rest of the sentence by commas.

EXAMPLES.

"She was tumbled early, by accident or design, into a spacious closet of good old English reading, without much selection or prohibition, and browsed at will upon that fair and wholesome pasturage."—*Lamb*.

"He [Sheridan] who, in less than thirty years afterward, held senates enchained by his eloquence and audiences fascinated by his wit, was, by common consent both of parent and preceptor, pronounced a most impenetrable dunce."—*Moore*.

"It is clear that Addison's serious attention, during his residence at the university, was almost entirely concentrated on Latin poetry."—*Macaulay*.

REMARKS.

1. A distinction should be made between parenthetical words and parenthetical expressions.

   a. Parenthetical words can be omitted without destroying the sense. See examples under Rule IV.

   b. Parenthetical expressions obstruct the flow of the sentence, but can not be omitted without either destroying the sense, or changing the meaning intended to be conveyed. See examples given above.

2. When parenthetical expressions are short, or closely connected with the rest of the sentence, it is better to omit punctuation marks.

3. **Writers differ** very much in omitting or using commas in parenthetical expressions. It is sometimes immaterial whether punctuation marks are used or not, but, in many cases, there are few rules so well adapted to bring out the meaning of the writer.

RULE VI. *Inverted Expressions.*—Expressions which are not in their natural order, are frequently separated from the rest of the sentence by a comma.

EXAMPLES.

"In everything that relates to science, I am a whole Encyclopædia behind the rest of the world." —*Lamb.*

"In all unhappy marriages I have seen, the great cause of evil has proceeded from slight occasions."—*Steele.*

REMARKS.

1. The natural order of the first sentence is, I am a whole Encyclopædia behind the rest of the world in everything that relates to science.

2. When the inverted expression is closely connected with what follows, the commas should be omitted; as,—

"Of Addison's childhood we know little."—*Macaulay.*

"That inward man I love that's lined with virtue."—*Beaumont and Fletcher.*

RULE VII. *Short Quotations.*—Short quotations should be separated from what precedes by a comma.

EXAMPLES.

The Italians say, "Good company in a journey makes the way to seem shorter."

A writer in *Lippincott's Magazine* says, " It is the little courtesies that make up the sum of a happy home."

Schiller has said, " Men's words are ever bolder than their deeds."

REMARKS.

1. An expression resembling a quotation should be preceded by a comma; as, "Therefore the question still returns, What is the First Principle of all things?"

2. Quotations and general statements introduced by *that* are frequently preceded by a comma; as, "Tacitus says of Agricola, that he governed his family, which many find to be a harder task than to govern a province."—*Arthur Helps.*

3. When single words or a part of a sentence are quoted, a comma should not be used; as, "His wife was a domesticated, kind-hearted old soul, who had come with him 'from the queen city of the world,' which, it seemed, was Philadelphia."—*Dickens.*

4. Quotation divided. "A man could not set his foot down," says Cortes, "unless on the corpse of an Indian."—*Prescott.*

5. When the quotation is a long one, it should be preceded by a colon.

RULE VIII. *Person or Thing Addressed.*— The name of the person or thing addressed, together with its modifying words, should be separated from the rest of the sentence by commas.

EXAMPLES.

"Now, Macaulay, when I am gone, you'll be sorry that you never heard me speak."—*Sydney Smith.*

"Why, Romeo, art thou mad?"—*Shakespeare.*

"My lords, we are called upon, as members of this house, as men, as Christians, to protest against such horrible barbarity!"—*Pitt.*

REMARK.

When strong emotion is expressed, an exclamation point should be used; as, "O Hamlet! thou hast cleft my heart in twain."—*Shakespeare.*

RULE IX. *Participial Clauses.*—Participial clauses, having no grammatical connection with the rest of the sentence, should be separated from what follows, and, if they do not commence a sentence, from what precedes, by commas.

EXAMPLES.

"Success being now hopeless, preparations were made for a retreat."—*Alison.*

"Such being their general idea of the gods, we can now easily understand the habitual tone of their feelings towards what was beautiful in nature."—*Ruskin.*

REMARK.

Being or *having been* is usually the sign of a participial clause.

Rule X. *Verb Omitted.*—When a verb, previously used, is omitted, a comma usually takes its place.

EXAMPLES.

"Histories make men wise; poets, witty; the mathematics, subtle; natural philosophy, deep; moral, grave; logic and rhetoric, able to contend."—*Bacon.*

"Chaucer painted persons; Spenser, qualities."

REMARKS.

1. When the comma takes the place of an omitted verb, the main clauses or numbers should be separated by semicolons.
2. Sometimes a comma does not take the place of an omitted verb; as, "Some books are to be tasted, others to be swallowed, and some few to be chewed and digested."—*Bacon.*

"Reading maketh a full man, conference a ready man, and writing an exact man."—*Bacon.*

Rule XI. *Appositives.*—A noun in apposition and its modifiers should be separated by commas from the rest of the sentence.

EXAMPLES.

"When death, the great Reconciler, has come, it is never our tenderness we repent of but our severity."—*George Eliot.*

"The exploits of Mercury himself, the god of cunning, may be easily imagined to surpass everything achieved by profaner hands."—*Leigh Hunt.*

REMARKS.

1. An appositive is a word, placed by the side of some other word to explain or characterize it.
2. The comma should be omitted,—
   a. When two nouns without modifiers are in apposition; as, Cicero the orator was born near Arpinum. If the sentence was, Cicero, the greatest of Roman orators, was born near Arpinum, commas would be necessary.
   b. When a noun and a pronoun are in apposition; as, Mercury himself surpassed everything achieved by profaner hands.
   c. When two pronouns are in apposition; as, He himself did this.
   d. Between the parts of a person's name; as, George William Curtis.
3. In annexing titles to a person's name, whether the titles are abbreviated or written in full, commas must be used; as, Richard Whately, D. D., Archbishop of Dublin.

RULE XII. *Words in Pairs.*—Words in pairs should have a comma between each pair.

EXAMPLES.

"In all the characters, patriots and tyrants, haters and lovers, the frown and sneer of Harold were discernible in an instant."—*Macaulay.*

"Liberty and union, now and forever, one and inseparable."—*Webster.*

RULE XIII. *Unconnected Words.*—When two words, of the same part of speech, are not connected by a conjunction, a comma should be placed between them.

EXAMPLES.

"He had in himself a radiant, living spring of generous and manly action."—*Burke.*

"A still, small voice."—*Kings.*

"Where sits our sulky, sullen dame,
Gathering her brows like gathering storm,
Nursing her wrath to keep it warm."—*Burns.*

REMARKS.

1. When two **nouns**, the subjects of a verb, **are not connected by a conjunction, a comma** should be placed **between the two words and also after the second**; as, "Indignation, expostulation, were powerless upon him as a mist upon a rock."—*Macdonald.*

2. When **two adjectives come together, the** first qualifying the second **adjective and also the noun, a** comma should **not be** used; as, A beautiful white horse.

3. **A word** repeated **for emphasis** usually has a punctuation mark before and after it; as,—

"Water, water, everywhere,
Nor any drop to drink."—*Coleridge.*

"Verily, verily, I say unto you, He that believeth on me, the works that I do shall he do also."—*John xiv. 12.*

RULE XIV. *A Series of Words.*—1. When a series of words, **of the same part of** speech, are connected by *and*, *or*, ***nor*, they should** not be separated from each other by **punctuation** marks.

"The fruits and flowers and shrubs sent forth grateful perfumes."—*Irving.*

Some writers place a comma before each *and*. This, however, is not necessary.

2. When a conjunction is used only with the last word in the series, a comma should be placed before the conjunction and between the other words.

The fruits, flowers, and shrubs sent forth grateful perfumes.

3. When the conjunctions are omitted, a comma should be placed between each word and also at the end of the series.

The fruits, flowers, shrubs, sent forth grateful perfumes.

REMARKS.

1. When the last word in the series precedes only a single word, the comma should be omitted; as, "A refined, thoughtful, warm-hearted, pure-souled Englishman."

2. When two words or expressions are connected by *or*, the latter explaining the former, the explanatory word or expression should be separated from the rest of the sentence by a comma or commas; as, "The love of variety, or curiosity of seeing new things, which is the same, or at least a sister passion to it, seems woven into the frame of every son and daughter of Adam."—*Sterne.*

RULE XV. *Phrases and Clauses.*—Phrases and clauses, either with or without conjunctions, having a mutual relation to some other word in the sentence, should be separated from each other and from what follows by commas.

EXAMPLES.

"Purity of style, and an easy flow of numbers, are common to all Addison's Latin poems."—*Macaulay.*

"The unbought grace of life, the chief defense of nations, the nurse of manly sentiment and heroic enterprise, is gone."—*Burke.*

"The little that is known, and the circumstance that little is known, must be considered as honorable to him."—*Macaulay.*

"Books that you can carry to the fire, and hold readily in your hand, are the most useful after all."—*Dr. Johnson.*

REMARKS.

1. A phrase is one of the smaller divisions of a sentence, and consists of two or more words. Apart from the rest of the sentence, it is incomplete in meaning. It does not, like a clause, include a subject and a verb.

2. When two brief expressions are connected by a conjunction, it is better to omit punctuation marks; as, "Good company and good discourse are the very sinews of virtue."—*Izaak Walton.*

3. When words and phrases form a series, a conjunction being used only with the last phrase, they should be separated from each other and from what follows by commas; as, "Virtue, merit, and everything that is praiseworthy, will be made the subject of ridicule and buffoonery."—*Addison.*

RULE XVI. *Logical Subject.*—When the logical subject ends with a verb, or is separated into parts by commas, or is unusually long, a comma should be placed **between** the logical subject and the main verb.

EXAMPLES.

"**This** imaginary promise **of** divine aid thus **mysteriously** given, appeared to **him** at present in still greater progress of fulfillment."—*Irving.*

"**The** voice of **praise**, too, coming **from** those to whom we had thought ourselves unknown, has a magic about it that must be felt **to be** understood." —*Charles Lever.*

"Those **who can** put the best countenance **upon** the outrages **of this** nature which are offered them, are not without their secret anguish."—*Addison.*

REMARKS.

1. **The logical** subject consists of **the name of the** person or **thing, of which** something **is affirmed,** together with its modifying **words.** It is "the subject **according to** the real meaning or logic of the sentence."

2. **Some** writers always place **a comma** before the verb, when its subject consists of many **words.**

RULE **XVII.** *Contrasted Expressions.*—Contrasted expressions **or** comparisons should **be separated** by a comma.

EXAMPLES.

"**Of** the other two men, one was a species of giant, the other a sort of dwarf."—*Hugo.*

"The more I reflected upon it, the more important it appeared."—*Goldsmith.*

"As the hart **panteth** after the water brooks, **so** panteth my soul after thee, O God."—*Psalms*.

"Master books, but **do not let** them master you. **Read to live,** not live to read."—*Bulwer*.

REMARKS.

1. **When** the comparison is short and **the** words closely connected, the comma **may** be omitted.

2. When *so—that, so—as, rather—than, more—than*, connect expressions, the comma is usually omitted; **as,** "Ingratitude never **so** thoroughly pierces **the** human heart **as when it** proceeds from those in whose behalf **we** have been guilty **of** transgression."—*Fielding*.

When, however, **the expressions** themselves are divided **into smaller parts by commas, or** are unusually **long, they should be separated by** a comma; **as,—**

"So over-violent, or over-civil,
That every man with him was God or Devil."—*Dryden*.

3. When two short expressions **are united** by *as* or *than*, a comma should not **be** used; as,—

"He knew what's what, **and** that's as **high**
As metaphysic wit can **fly**."—*Butler*.

When, however, the expressions are long, **it is** better to use **a** comma; **as,** "I have **no** more pleasure **in** hearing **a** man attempting wit and failing, than in seeing a man trying to leap over **a ditch and** tumbling into **it**."—*Dr. Johnson*.

4. When **the first** expression is negative and **the** other affirmative, **a comma** should be placed between **the expressions and** before the negative **word, if** it does not commence **a sentence;** as, "The world generally gives **its** admiration, not to **the** man who does what nobody else even attempts to do, but to the man who **does best** what multitudes do well."
—*Macaulay*.

If, however, a finite verb immediately precedes the negative word, the comma should be omitted; as, "Our greatest glory is not in never falling, but in rising every time we fall."—*Confucius.*

Rule XVIII. *Numeral Figures.*—Arabic numbers should be separated into periods of three figures each, commencing at the right.

EXAMPLE.

2,509,909,456.

REMARK.

Dates should not be separated into periods; as, 1877.

Rule XIX. *Expressions at the End of Sentences.*—It is frequently necessary, at the end of a sentence, to separate an expression beginning with a preposition from the rest of the sentence, in order to avoid ambiguity.

EXAMPLES.

"He trudged along, unknowing what he sought,
And whistled as he went, for want of thought."—*Dryden.*

"Angling is always to be considered as a stick and a string, with a fly at one end and a fool at the other."—*Swift.*

GENERAL REMARK.

A comma should always be used, when it aids in bringing out the meaning of the writer, or in avoiding ambiguity.

THE SEMICOLON.

Rule I. *Long Sentences.*—When the smaller divisions of sentences are separated by commas, the main divisions should be separated by semicolons.

EXAMPLES.

"Sheridan, Pitt, and Fox all drank hard and worked hard; they were all great in the councils of the nation, but not one could rule his own household."—*London Athenæum.*

"Stiff in opinions, always in the wrong;
Was every thing by starts, and nothing long."—*Dryden.*

"Nor is it always in the most distinguished achievements that men's virtues or vices may be best discerned; but very often an action of small note, a short saying, or a jest, shall distinguish a person's real character more than the greatest sieges, or the most important battles."—*Plutarch.*

Rule II. *Expressions Complete in Themselves.*—Short expressions, complete in themselves but slightly connected in meaning, may be separated by semicolons.

EXAMPLES.

"We do not want precepts so much as patterns; an example is the softest and least invidious way of commanding."—*Pliny.*

"It is a beautiful thing to model a statue and give it life; to mould an intelligence and instil truth therein is still more beautiful."—*Hugo.*

"There are on every subject a few leading and fixed ideas; their tracks may be traced by your own genius as well as by reading."—*Sheridan.*

REMARK.

When *as* introduces an example, a semicolon should be placed before and a comma after it.

RULE III. *Series of Expressions.*—When several clauses follow each other in succession, having a common dependence on some part of the sentence, they should be separated from each other by semicolons, and from the clause on which they depend, by a comma.

EXAMPLE.

"If such men will make a firm and solemn pause, and meditate dispassionately on its importance; if they will contemplate it in all its attributes, and trace it to all its consequences, they will not hesitate to part with trivial objections to a constitution, the rejection of which would, in all probability, put a final period to the Union."—*Hamilton.*

REMARK.

Commas may be used instead of semicolons, when the clauses are short; as, "When public bodies are to be addressed on momentous occasions, when great interests are at stake, and strong passions excited, nothing is valuable in speech farther than it is connected with high intellectual and moral endowments."—*Webster.*

GENERAL REMARK.

When the members of a sentence seem to be loosely connected, they are frequently separated by semicolons.

EXAMPLES.

"Honest name is goodly; but he that hunteth only for that, is like him that hath rather seem warm than be warm."—*Sir Thomas Wyatt.*

"Some blemishes may undoubtedly be detected in his character; but the more carefully it is examined, the more will it appear sound in the noble parts."—*Macaulay.*

Some writers use commas in the examples given above in preference to semicolons, and usage varies so much among our best writers that it is impossible to lay down a general rule that will be applicable in all cases. If it is desirable to indicate a somewhat close connection between the members of a sentence, a comma should be used; if the connection is slight, it is better to use a semicolon.

THE COLON.

RULE I. *Long Sentences.*—When the smaller divisions of sentences are separated by semicolons, the main divisions should be separated by a colon.

EXAMPLES.

"Emulation is a dangerous passion to encourage, in some points, in young men; it is so linked with envy: if you reproach your son for not surpassing his school-fellows, he will hate those who are before him."—*Sheridan.*

"A man over ninety is a great comfort to all his elderly neighbors: he is a picket-guard at the extreme outpost; and the young folks of sixty and seventy feel that the enemy must get by him before he can come near the camp."—*O. W. Holmes.*

RULE II. *A Quotation.*—A colon should precede a long quotation. If, however, the quotation is short, it is better to use a comma.

EXAMPLES.

Socrates recommended to one of his disciples the following prayer: "O Jupiter, give us those things which are good for us, whether they are such things as we pray for, or such things as we do not pray for; and remove from us those things which are hurtful, though they are such things as we pray for."

When the Earl of Dudley took leave of Sydney Smith, on going from London to Yorkshire, he said: "You have been laughing at me constantly, Sydney, for the last seven years, and yet, in all that time, you never said a single thing to me that I wished unsaid."

REMARK.

1. When the quotation is long, or it begins a new paragraph, a dash is frequently placed after the colon.
2. When a direct quotation is introduced into the middle of a sentence, a comma should be used; as, "He was surprised, but replied, 'I am not the king, he is there,' pointing at the same time to a different part of the hall."—*Lingard.*

R<small>ULE</small> III. *Enumeration of Particulars.*—A colon should precede an enumeration of particulars, when they are formally introduced by *thus, following, as follows, this, these,* &c.

EXAMPLES.

"We hold these truths to be self-evident: that all men are created equal; that they are endowed by their Creator with inalienable rights: that among these are life, liberty, and the pursuit of happiness."—*Jefferson.*

"The penalty is graduated thus: the mildest, confiscation; the moderate, closing the shop; the severest, exposure."—*Lippincott's Magazine.*

REMARKS.

1. When the particulars are preceded by a colon, they are usually separated from each other by semicolons, as in the examples given above.
2. If the particulars are not introduced by *thus, following,* &c., they should be preceded by a semicolon; as, "Grammar is divided into four parts; Orthography, Etymology, Syntax, and Prosody."
3. When the particulars are preceded by a semicolon, they are usually separated from each other by commas.

4. Sometimes a comma and dash are used instead of a semicolon; as, "Grammar is divided into four parts,— Orthography, Etymology, Syntax, and Prosody.

GENERAL REMARK.

The colon is used by some writers to separate short expressions that are complete in themselves, but slightly connected in meaning.

EXAMPLES.

"But men are men: the best sometimes forget."
—*Shakespeare.*

"It [the Seine] is the wash-tub and summer bath-tub of its citizens; it was the birthplace of Paris, and it is too often the grave of her children." —*Lippincott's Magazine.*

If a conjunction is used, it is better to use a semicolon; as,—

"She cannot separate her name from his without lessening it; for it is equally incrusted with his greatness as with his faults."—*Lamartine.*

She cannot separate her name from his without lessening it: it is equally incrusted with his greatness as with his faults.

The colon is not as commonly used as formerly. A semicolon would be preferred by very many writers in all sentences similar to the examples given above. See Rule II. p. 23.

THE PERIOD.

RULE I. *Complete Sentences.*—A period should be placed at the end of a sentence, when it is complete in meaning and construction, and is declarative or imperative in its nature.

EXAMPLES.

"Swift boasted that he was never known to steal a hint."—*Macaulay.*

"But evil is wrought by want of thought,
As well as want of heart."—*Hood.*

"It is a great evil not to be able to bear an evil."
—*Bion.*

REMARK.

A period should always be placed after the **title of an** essay, oration, after a signature, an address of a **person, &c.**

RULE II. *Abbreviations.*—A period should be used after every abbreviation.

EXAMPLES.

Dr. Samuel **A. Jones. Mr. C. R.** Miller. Mrs. **T. S.** Applegate. Miss **Hattie E.** Knapp.

Esq., Esquire.	**Pro tem.,** for the time being.
Jan., January.	**Ans.,** Answer.
Mich., Michigan.	**D. D.,** Doctor of Divinity.
Hon., Honorable.	**B. C., before** Christ.

Rev., Reverend.   A. D., in the year of our Lord.
P., page; pp., pages.   A. M., Master of Arts.
Pres., President.   [tary.   M. C., Member of Congress.
Rec. Sec., Recording Secre- No., in number, number.
N. Y., New York.   Co., County.
              &c. or etc., and so forth.

REMARKS.

1. It should be remembered that the period thus used, simply indicates an abbreviation, and that punctuation marks are to be used, in addition to the period, when required. When a word, written in full, requires a punctuation mark after it, the same punctuation mark should be used after the word, when it is abbreviated; as, Adrian, Michigan, January 5, 1877; Adrian, Mich., Jan. 5, 1877.

2. Some proper names are not abbreviations, and consequently a period should not be used; as, Ben Jonson, Fred Knapp. When Ben. stands for Benjamin, and Fred. for Frederick, a period should be used.

3. When numerals are represented by the letters of the alphabet, periods are placed after them; as, Gen. vii. 1, 7, 8.

4. In numbering pages, no mark should be placed after 1, 2, 3, 4, &c.

5. When a letter, used as an abbreviation, is doubled to indicate the plural, the period should be placed after the last letter; as, pp. for pages, LL. D. for Doctor of Laws.

6. In abbreviating words, sometimes the first letters are used, sometimes the first and last, and sometimes the first and some letter near the middle of the word; as, Ala. for Alabama, Chas. for Charles, Wm. for William, MS. for manuscript.

7. A list of abbreviations will be found at the close of any good dictionary.

INTERROGATION POINT.

Rule I. *Direct Question.*—A direct question must be followed by an interrogation point.

EXAMPLES.

" Who ever knew truth put to the worse, in a free and open encounter?"—*Milton.*

"Are you good men and true?"—*Shakespeare.*

EXCLAMATION POINT.

RULE I. *Strong Emotion.*—The exclamation point is used after expressions denoting strong emotion.

EXAMPLES.

"Discipline of mind! say rather starvation, confinement, torture, annihilation."—*Macaulay.*

"My valor is certainly going! it is sneaking off! I feel it oozing out, as it were, at the palms of my hands."—*Sheridan.*

"How sharper than a serpent's tooth it is
To have a thankless child!"—*Shakespeare.*

REMARK.

To express an unusual degree of emotion, more than one exclamation point may be used.

RULE II. *Interjections.*—All interjections except *O* may be followed by an exclamation point.

EXAMPLES.

"But, alas! to make me
The fixed figure of the time, for scorn
To point his slow unmoving finger at."—*Shakespeare.*

"Oh! blessed temper, whose unclouded ray
Can make to-morrow cheerful as to-day."—*Pope.*

"O thou invisible spirit of wine, if thou hast no name to be known by, let us call thee devil!"—*Shakespeare.*

REMARKS.

1. When the connection between the interjection and what follows is very close, it is sometimes better to put the exclamation point at the end of the sentence; as,—

"Oh for that ancient spirit
Which curbed the Senate's will!"—*Macaulay.*

2. When it is desirable to express strong feeling throughout an entire sentence, the exclamation point should be placed at the end; as,—

"Ho, trumpets, sound a war-note!
Ho, lictors, clear the way!"—*Macaulay.*

RULE III. *Address.*—Expressions of address, when emphatic, may be followed by an exclamation point.

EXAMPLES.

"Lord! what music hast thou provided for the saints in heaven, when thou affordest bad men such music [music of the nightingale] on earth."—*Izaak Walton.*

"Hail, candle-light! without disparagement to sun or moon, the kindest luminary of the three."—*Lamb.*

"Sweet Auburn! loveliest village of the plain."—*Goldsmith.*

"Ah! happy years! once more who would not be a boy."—*Byron.*

THE DASH.

Rule I. *Broken Sentences.*—When a sentence is broken off abruptly, or there is an unexpected change in the sentiment, or hesitation is to be indicated, a dash should be used.

EXAMPLES.

Prince.—" I tell you what, my cousin Buckingham,—"
Buck.—" What, my gracious lord?"—*Shakespeare.*

" I only feel—Farewell—Farewell!"—*Byron.*

" You will think me foolish;—but—but—may it not be that some invisible angel has been attracted by the simplicity and good faith with which our children set about their undertaking? May he not have spent an hour of his immortality in playing with those dear little souls?"—*Hawthorne.*

" Men will wrangle for religion; write for it; fight for it; die for it; anything but—*live for it.*"—*Colton.*

Rule II. *Concluding Clause.*—When several expressions follow each other in succession, having a common dependence on the concluding part of the sentence, a dash is frequently placed before the clause on which they depend.

EXAMPLES.

" If you think it a crime in this writer that his language has not been braided and festooned as elegantly as it might be; that he has not pinched the miserable plaits of his phraseology, nor placed his patches and feathers with that correctness of millinery which became him,—then find a civil and obliging verdict against the printer!"—*Curran.*

" To foster industry, to promote union, to cherish religious peace,—these were the honest purposes of Lord Baltimore during his long supremacy."—*Bancroft.*

REMARKS.

1. A dash is sometimes used to give prominence or emphasis to an emphatic conclusion; as, " Fortune, friends, kindred, home,—all were gone."—*Prescott.*

2. When such words as *namely, that is*, &c., are omitted, a dash is sometimes used; as, " Many actions, like the Rhone, have two sources,—one pure, and the other impure."—*Hare.*

3. When a word or an expression is repeated for emphasis, a dash should be placed before it; as, " It is this, I conjure Your Lordships, for your honor, for the honor of the nation, for the honor of human nature, now intrusted to your care, —it is this duty that the Commons of England, speaking through us, claims at your hands."—*Sheridan.*

RULE III. *Subjects.*—When the subject of a general statement, or the subject of a quotation, is in the same paragraph with the subject-matter, a dash should separate the subject from what follows.

EXAMPLES.

The Bible.—"A person who professes to be a critic in the niceties of the English language ought to have the Bible at his fingers' ends."—*Macaulay*.

Letter-Writing.—" Common interests are necessary to give permanent stability to epistolary connections. We may love a man dearly, and yet find no time to write ten lines to him."—*From the German of Rudolph Lindau*.

REMARKS.

1. A subject is a word or expression about which some statement is made.

2. A dash should be placed between a quotation and the author from whom the quotation is taken.

3. When a question and an answer are in the same paragraph, a dash is frequently inserted between the two; as, "Saw you my lord?"—" No, lady."

4. When *as, thus, as follows*, &c., introduce an example or a quotation, a dash should be placed after the comma or colon, if what follows commences a new paragraph; as,—

"All we possess, and use not on the road,
Adds to the burden we must bear."—*Goethe*.

RULE IV. *Letters or Figures Omitted.*—When letters or figures are omitted, a dash should be used to indicate the omission.

EXAMPLES.

" Why, to comfort me, must Alice W——n be a goblin?"—*Lamb*.

Mark xi. 1-10. Gen. v. 3-9.

REMARK.

3–9 is equivalent to 3, 4, 5, 6, 7, 8, 9.

GENERAL REMARK.

The dash is frequently used to give prominence or emphasis to an expression.

EXAMPLES.

"In the quiet air, there was a sound of distant singing,—shepherd voices."—*Dickens.*

"Wealth has its temptations,—so has power."—*Robertson.*

"The poorest man may in his cottage bid defiance to all the force of the crown. It may be frail; its roof may shake; the wind may blow through it; the storms may enter, the rains may enter,—but the king of England cannot enter! all his forces dare not cross the threshold of the ruined tenement."—*Pitt.*

RULE V. *Parenthesis.*—Two dashes are sometimes used instead of the usual marks of parenthesis.

EXAMPLES.

"A yellow claw—the very same that had clawed together so much wealth—poked itself out of the coach window, and dropt some copper coins upon the ground."—*Hawthorne.*

"Jackson—the omniscient Jackson he was called—was of this period. He had the reputation of possessing more multifarious knowledge than any man of his time."—*Lamb*.

REMARKS.

1. When the sentence, without the parenthesis, would require a comma where the dashes are used, each dash should be preceded by a comma; as, "See that aged couple,—a sad sight, truly,—John Proctor, and his wife Elizabeth."—*Hawthorne*.

2. If the parenthetical expression is a question or expresses emotion, an interrogation or an exclamation point should be placed before the second dash; as, "The laurel of the hero—alas for humanity that it should be so!—grows best on the battle field."

MARKS OF PARENTHESIS.

RULE I. *Parenthesis.*—When an expression breaks the connection between the different parts of a sentence, and might be omitted without affecting the sense or the construction, it should be inclosed in parenthetical marks.

EXAMPLES.

" Of all sound of all bells (bells, the music nighest bordering heaven) most solemn and touching is the peal which rings out the Old Year."—*Lamb.*

" The tuneful Nine (so sacred legends tell)
First waked their heavenly lyre these scenes to tell!"
—*Campbell.*

" Their intellectual wardrobe (to confess fairly) has few whole pieces in it."—*Lamb.*

REMARKS.

1. When parenthetical marks are used, it is sometimes necessary to use additional marks.

  a. When the sentence, without the parenthesis, requires a punctuation mark where the parenthetical marks are used, the punctuation mark should be placed after the last mark of the parenthesis; as,—
  " Know then this truth (enough for man to know),
  ' Virtue alone is happiness below.'"—*Pope.*

b. Sometimes the parenthesis requires a punctuation mark before the last mark of the parenthesis; as, "Spill not the morning (the quintessence of the day!) in recreations."—*Thomas Fuller.*

c. When a punctuation mark immediately precedes the last mark of the parenthesis, and a punctuation mark is also needed where the parenthetical marks are used, it should be placed before the first mark of the parenthesis; as, "F. was the most gentlemanly of oilmen. He had two Latin words almost constantly in his mouth, (how odd sounds Latin from an oilman's lips!) which my better knowledge since has enabled me to correct."—*Lamb.*

2. An interrogation point inclosed in parenthetical marks (?) implies that an assertion is doubtful.

3. An exclamation point inclosed within parenthetical marks (!) expresses irony or contempt.

4. Parenthetical marks are not as frequently used as formerly, the comma and dash being often preferred.

BRACKETS.

RULE I. *Quoted Passage.*—When words are inserted by another into a quoted passage, either to correct a mistake or explain the meaning, they should be inclosed in brackets.

EXAMPLES.

"A variety of pleasing objects meet [meets] the eye."

"'My dear lady,' returned the schoolmaster [Mr. Graham], 'when I have on good grounds made up my mind to a thing, I always feel as if I had promised God to do it; and indeed it amounts to the same thing very nearly. Such a resolve, then, is not to be unmade, except on equally good grounds with those upon which it was made.'"—*George Macdonald.*

REMARKS.

1. Punctuation marks are sometimes required, when the brackets are used. The same remarks apply to the brackets that apply to parenthetical marks.

2. In reporting speeches, brackets are used, when words are introduced by the reporter which do not form a part of the speech; as,—

"We would have our Union to be a union of hearts, and we would have our Constitution obeyed, not merely because of force that compels obedience, but obeyed because the people love the principles of the Constitution [long continued applause], and to-day, if I am called to the work to which Abraham Lincoln was called sixteen years ago, it is under brighter skies and more favorable auspices. [Applause.] I do hope, I do fervently believe, that, by the aid of divine Providence, we may do something in this day of peace, by works of peace, towards re-establishing, in the hearts of our countrymen, a real, a hearty attachment to the Constitution as it is, and to the Union as it is. [Long continued applause]. —PRESIDENT HAYES.—*Chicago Tribune.*

3. Parenthetical marks are frequently used instead of brackets.

QUOTATION MARKS.

Rule I. *Direct Quotation.*—When the exact words of another are given, they should be inclosed in quotation marks.

EXAMPLES.

"He had the longest tongue and the shortest temper of any man, high or low, I ever met with."
—*Wilkie Collins.*

Prescott, in his "Conquest of Mexico," tells us that intemperance among the Aztecs "was punished in the young with death, and in older persons with loss of rank and confiscation of property."

REMARKS.

1. When the exact words of another are not given, quotation marks should not be used; as,—
Longfellow says,—
   "Deeds are better things than words are."
Longfellow somewhere says that deeds are better than words.

2. When words are quoted from a foreign language, they should be printed in italics, and the quotation marks omitted; as, "They have their good glebe lands *in manu*, and care not much to rake into title deeds."—*Lamb.*

3. When words are to be italicized, a straight mark should be drawn underneath the words.

4. When a quotation is followed by a comma, semicolon, colon, or period, the punctuation mark should be placed within the quotation marks; as, "Mr. M'Adam writes sometimes with genuine humor, and an occasional entirely original simile shows evidence of the possession of what phrenologists call the faculty of 'comparison;' but the charm of the book is its rare perspicacity."—*Harper's Magazine*.

5. When a quotation is followed by an exclamation or an interrogation point, the punctuation mark should be placed within the quotation marks, if it forms a part of the quotation; as, "I feel almost like groaning, when a young mother shows me some marvel of embroidery or machine-stitching, saying triumphantly, 'There, I did every stitch of that myself!'"—*Scribner's Monthly*.

6. When a quotation is followed by an exclamation or an interrogation point, the punctuation mark should be placed outside of the quotation marks, if it belongs to the whole sentence and not to the quotation; as, "We wonder what Handel would have said to Mozart's scoring of 'I know that my Redeemer liveth'!"—*Atlantic Monthly*. "Why cannot we hear, for instance, the wonderful curioso, 'He gave his back to the smiters,' that forms the second part of the air, 'He was despised,' and the duet for contralto and tenor, 'O death where is thy sting'?"—*Atlantic Monthly*.

RULE II. *Titles of Books.*—Titles of books are generally inclosed in quotation marks.

EXAMPLES.

Morris's "Story of Sigurd."—*Scribner's Monthly*.
"The Mikado's Empire."—*N. A. Review*.
"Daniel Deronda."—*Contemporary Review*.
The Rev. W. W. Capes's history of "The Early Roman Empire."—*Appleton's Journal*.

REMARKS.

1. The names of magazines and papers are generally printed in italics; as, *The Atlantic, N. Y. Nation, Fraser's Magazine, Appleton's Journal, Nature, Popular Science Monthly.*

2. In examining *The Atlantic, Nation, Scribner's Monthly, Harper's, Appleton's Magazine, Lippincott's, Popular Science Monthly, Galaxy, Eclectic, N. A. Review, New Englander, London Quarterly, British Quarterly, Westminster Review, Edinburgh Review, Contemporary Review, The Fortnightly Review,* we find that thirteen of these use quotation marks, and four use italics, in referring to the titles of books; eleven use italics, and six use quotation marks, in referring to magazines and papers.

RULE III. *A Quotation within a Quotation.*—When there is a quotation within a quotation, single marks should be used in addition to double marks.

EXAMPLES.

"Who was the blundering idiot who said that 'fine words butter no parsnips.' Half the parsnips of society are served and rendered palatable with no other sauce."—*Thackeray.*

"There is a small but ancient fraternity, known as the Order of Gentlemen. It is a grand old order. A poet has said that Christ founded it; that he was 'the first true gentleman that ever lived.'"—*Winthrop.*

REMARKS.

1. Sometimes the quotation within a quotation has a word or phrase that is quoted. The word or phrase must be inclosed in double marks.

2. In quoting Scripture, it is customary to place only double marks at the beginning and end of the quotation; as, "And Jesus, moved with compassion, put forth his hand, and touched him, and saith unto him, I will; be thou clean." —*Mark i. 41.*

RULE IV. *Paragraphs.*—When several paragraphs are quoted in succession, double marks should be placed at the beginning of each paragraph, and at the end of the entire quotation.

EXAMPLE.

" The children woke. The little girl was the first to open her eyes.

" The waking of children is like the unclosing of flowers, a perfume seems to exhale from those fresh young souls. Georgette, twenty months old, the youngest of the three, who was still a nursing baby in the month of May, raised her little head, sat up in her cradle, looked at her feet, and began to chatter.

" A ray of morning fell across her crib; it would have been difficult to decide which was the rosiest, Georgette's foot or Aurora."—*Hugo.*

REMARKS.

1. A paragraph usually consists of several sentences. It begins on a new line, and is distinguished by a blank space on the left, at the commencement of the paragraph.

2. When parts of a quotation are omitted, use several stars to indicate the omission (* * * *), or place double marks at the beginning and end of each detached part of the quotation.

THE APOSTROPHE.

Rule I. *Letters Omitted.*—The apostrophe is used to indicate the omission of a letter or letters.

EXAMPLES.

"O Marcia, O my sister, still there's hope!"—*Addison.*

"Thou knowest 'tis common; all, that live, must die, Passing through nature to eternity."—*Shakespeare.*

REMARK.

The apostrophe is made like a comma, but is placed above the line.

Rule II. *Possession.*—The apostrophe is used to denote possession.

EXAMPLES.

Taine's " English Literature." Rawlinson's " Ancient Monarchies."

REMARKS.

1. The apostrophe and *s* should be used with nouns in the singular, even when the word ends in *s* or *x;* as,—

"Dickens's Works."—*Appleton's Journal.*
"Cox's General History of Greece."—*Harper's Magazine.*
"Evans's observations."—*Edinburgh Review.*
"Mr. Hayes's responsibility."—*N. Y. Nation.*

In addition to the periodicals given above, *The Atlantic, Scribner's Monthly, Lippincott's Magazine, Popular Science Monthly, Galaxy, N. A. Review, London Quarterly, British Quarterly, Fortnightly Review,* use the additional *s*. The *Westminster* omits the additional *s*. In the *Contemporary* and *Edinburgh Review*, the *s* is used by some writers and omitted by others.

2. In the plural of nouns, the apostrophe and *s* are used to denote possession, when the word does not end in *s;* as, men's deeds. If the word ends in *s*, the apostrophe only is used; as, my neighbors' house.

3. The apostrophe should not be used before *s* in ours, yours, hers, theirs, its.

THE HYPHEN.

Rule I. *Compound* **Words.**—The hyphen is used to connect the parts of a compound word.

EXAMPLES.

"My household-gods plant a terrible fixed foot, and are not to be rooted up without blood."—*Lamb.*

"The breezy call of incense-breathing morn."—*Gray.*

REMARKS.

1. A compound word is formed by placing together two simple words.
2. Sometimes several words are connected together by hyphens; as, "He had a lively touch-and-go-away with him, very pleasant and engaging I admit."—*Wilkie Collins.*
3. When a compound word comes into very general use, the hyphen is sometimes omitted; as, railroad, steamboat, bookstore.
4. To-day, to-night, to-morrow, should always be written with a hyphen.
5. When there is any doubt whether two words should be united by a hyphen or written as one word, some standard dictionary should be consulted. It will, however, be found that even dictionaries differ somewhat in the use and omission of the hyphen in compound words. In order to preserve some uniformity in spelling and in the formation of

compound words, every writer should make either Webster or Worcester the final authority.

Rule II. *Prefixes.*—When a prefix ends in a vowel, and the word to which it is joined commences with a vowel, they should be separated by a hyphen.

EXAMPLES.

Re-admit, co-ordinate, pre-existence, pre-eminent.

REMARKS.

1. A prefix is a letter, syllable, or word, placed before some word, thus forming a new word.
2. If, instead of two vowels, a vowel and a consonant come together, the prefix and the word to which it is joined should usually be written as one word; as, rewrite, predetermine.
3. Vice-president, and most words with *vice* as a prefix, should be written with a hyphen.
4. Some writers use the diæresis instead of the hyphen. With prefixes it is better to use the hyphen; but in other words containing two vowels that do not form a diphthong, the diæresis should be used; as, Zoölogy.

Rule III. *Division of Words.*—When it is necessary to write part of a word at the end of a line and part at the beginning of the next line, the division should be made at the end of a syllable, and the parts should be connected by a hyphen, at the end of the line.

EXAMPLE.

"Knowledge is of two kinds. We know a subject ourselves, or we know where we can find information upon it."—*Dr. Johnson.*

REMARKS.

1. It is better to divide a word as near the middle as possible.

2. When two words, one at the end of a line and the other at the commencement of the following line, are separated by a punctuation mark, it should be placed at the end of the line, and never at the beginning.

MISCELLANEOUS MARKS.

I. *Two Commas* (") indicate that the word under which they are placed is to be repeated.

        Charles Harrison, Adrian, Mich.
        Clinton Hardy,   "   "

II. *The Caret* (∧) indicates that something is written above the line that forms a part of the sentence. It is only used in writing.

"His life of danger and hardship ^was^ *uncheered by hope, his death* ^n^ *unoticed."*

III. *Marks of Ellipsis* (—, ..., * * * *) indicate the omission of letters, words, or sentences.

1. "I was the true descendant of those old W—s."—*Lamb.*

2. "I have a belief of my own, ... that by desiring what is perfectly good, even when we don't quite know what it is, ... we are a part of a divine power against evil, widening the skirts of light, and making the struggle with darkness narrower."—*George Eliot.*

Four words are omitted where the first dots are, and five where the second are.

3. "My lov'd, my honour'd, much respected friend!
   * * * * * * * * *
   To you I sing, in simple Scottish lays,
   The lowly train in life's sequester'd scene,
   The native feeling strong, the guileless ways;
   What Aiken in his cottage would have been."
   —*Burns.*

In the above, three lines are omitted.

IV. *Leaders* (......) are used to indicate a connection between words at the beginning of the line and what is at the end of the line.

Winnowed Wheat................*Nellie R. Luck.*
Dreams, a Poem................*Octa E. Wise.*

V. In writing, one line drawn under a word indicates that it is to be printed in italics; two lines, in small capitals; three lines, in capitals.

VI. *Marks of Reference* are used to refer to notes at the bottom of the page, or to remarks in the margin. They are the following:—

The Star (*), the Dagger (†), the Double Dagger (‡), the Section (§), Parallel Lines (||), the Paragraph (¶).

The above marks are given in the order in which they are used.

The Paragraph (¶) is also used, in written compositions, to denote that what follows should commence a new line.

Capitals.

INTRODUCTION.

It has been the custom among some writers to commence every important word with a capital, so that some printed productions have fairly bristled with capitalized words; as,—

"Modern authors have with unwearied Pains made many useful Searches into the weak Sides of the Ancients, and given us a comprehensive Lift of them."—*Swift*.

"There were a Race of Men who delighted to nibble at the Superfluities and Excrescences of Books."—*Swift*.

The custom of commencing all nouns with a capital is still prevalent among the Germans of the present day.

It is a somewhat interesting fact that the use and value of capitals has been subject to a rise and fall in the literary market, written productions during some centuries abounding in them, while in other centuries they have, in a great measure, been discarded, and have become comparative strangers in English composition.

In the early part of this century, there was a tendency to use them to an inconsiderate extent, owing principally to German imitators like Carlyle and others, who adopted, in a somewhat modified form, the German method of capitalizing words. Just at present there seems to be a reaction setting in, and there is a tendency among some of our leading publishing houses to dispense with their use as much as possible. In democratic America, there has always been a somewhat unreasonable fear of official titles, and when they are used, they are frequently belittled with small letters. This has had a tendency to encourage the use of small letters in many words that should properly commence with capitals.

There is no doubt that a judicious use of capitals assists the eye very much in reading what another has written, and in understanding a writer's meaning. While, on the other hand, an injudicious use lessens their value, and disfigures a printed page.

Although the taste and judgment of each writer may be consulted in the capitalization of some words to which he may assign a special meaning, there are a number of well established principles, sanctioned by long usage, that should govern all writers in the use of capital letters.

CAPITALS.

Rule I. *Sentences.*—The first word of every sentence should commence with a capital.

EXAMPLES.

" The price we challenge for ourselves is given us."—*Schiller.*

" The elder brother of Franklin ventured to start a newspaper, though warned that America could never support two newspapers."— *William Russel.*

" Trust in yourself, and you have learnt to live."—*Goethe.*

REMARKS.

1. A sentence is an assemblage of words making complete sense, and followed by a period. Sometimes a sentence has an interrogation or an exclamation point at its close; as,—

" For of the wholly common is man made,
And custom is his nurse!"—*Schiller.*

2. Any expression that is equivalent to a sentence should commence with a capital; as, Very affectionately. Price $5.00.

3. As a period indicates the close of a sentence, the word following the period should commence with a capital; as, " The little soul is like a vapor that hovers around a marshy lake. It never rises on the green hill, lest the winds meet it there."—*Ossian.*

If, however, a period is used to indicate an abbreviation, it should not be followed by a capital, unless it is at the close of a sentence, or the word that follows it requires a capital; as, In Germany, the degrees of M. D., LL. D., and Ph. D. are only gained after passing a severe examination.

4. Although a capital is generally used after an interrogation or an exclamation point, as they usually indicate the close of a sentence, this is not always the case; as,—

"How poor! how rich! how abject! how august!
How complicate! how wonderful is man!
How passing wonder He who made him such!
Who centered in our make such strange extremes!"
—Young.

RULE II. *Poetry.*—The first word of every line of poetry should commence with a capital.

EXAMPLES.

"There is a day of sunny rest
  For every dark and troubled night;
And grief may bide an evening guest,
  But joy shall come with early light."—*Bryant.*

"But far more numerous was the herd of such,
Who think too little and who talk too much."—*Dryden.*

RULE III. *Persons and Places.*—Names of persons, countries, cities, islands, rivers, mountains, &c., should commence with capitals.

EXAMPLES.

"The finest thief of old history is the pirate who made that famous answer to Alexander, in which he said that the conqueror was only the mightier thief of the two."—*Leigh Hunt.*

America, France, London, New York, West Indies, Hudson, Rhine, Rocky Mountains, Mount Vernon, Pacific.

REMARKS.

1. When North, South, East, &c., refer to political or geographical divisions, they should commence with capitals; as, "But sectional bitterness has in a great measure passed away; the fatal cause of discord between North and South has been removed."

When these words refer merely to the points of the compass, they should be written with small letters.

2. Words derived from the names of persons should commence with capitals; as, Socratic, Platonic, Elizabethan.

When words derived from the names of persons or places lose their individual character, and are used as common words, they should commence with small letters; as, godlike, hector, turkey, china-ware, laconic.

3. Heaven and hell are written with small letters in the Bible. Satan is always printed with a capital, but devil commences with a small letter, unless it stands for Satan; as, "Then was Jesus led up of the Spirit into the wilderness to be tempted of the devil."—Mat. iv. 1.

RULE IV. *Nations.*—The names of nations, or words derived from the names of nations, should commence with capitals.

EXAMPLES.

"'Simply to be poor,' says my favorite Greek historian, 'was not held scandalous by the wise Athenians; but highly so, to owe that poverty to our own indiscretion.'"—*Fielding.*

American, German, French, Latins, Americanize, Latinize, Hellenize.

REMARK.

Italics and Italicize are frequently written with small letters.

RULE V. *Sects and Parties.*—The names of religious sects and political parties should commence with capitals.

EXAMPLES.

Christian, Mohammedan, Lutheran, Catholic, Protestant, Episcopal, Presbyterian, Baptist, Unitarian.

Republican, Federalist, Democrat, Whig, Tory, Radical.

REMARKS.

1. When republican, radical, &c., are used as common words, and not as the names of political parties, they should commence with small letters; as, republican institutions, radical measures.

2. Some writers use small letters, when referring to political parties. If, however, it is incorrect to write Congregational, Methodist, with small letters, why is it not incorrect to commence Republican, Whig, with small letters?

3. Church should be written with a capital, when it refers to a religious sect; as, the Episcopal Church, meaning the whole body of Christians belonging to that denomination. When the word refers to a place of worship, it should commence with a small letter.

RULE VI. *Months and Days.*—The names of months and days should commence with capitals.

EXAMPLES.

"No one ever regarded the first of January with indifference. It is that from which all date their time, and count upon what is left. It is the nativity of our common Adam."—*Lamb.*

February, March, April, May; Monday, Tuesday, Wednesday, Sunday, Good Friday, Easter.

REMARK.

Spring, summer, autumn, winter, should be written with small letters.

Rule VII. *Titles of Books.*—All the words, with the exception of articles, conjunctions, and prepositions, in the titles of books, should commence with a capital.

EXAMPLES.

Forsyth's "Life of Cicero." "The Fall of the Roman Republic," Rev. C. Merivale.

REMARKS.

1. It is just as necessary to capitalize the title of a book, as it is the name of a person.
2. The title of an oration, essay, article for a newspaper, or of any written production, follows the same rule as the title of a book.
3. Names of sacred writings should always be capitalized; as, Bible, Old and New Testament, the Scriptures, Acts, Revelation, Gospel of John, Koran, Vedas.

Rule VIII. *Title-Pages.*—The title-pages of books are generally printed entirely with capitals. The title-page of any book will illustrate this rule.

REMARKS.

1. This rule concerns more especially the printer.
2. The first word of a chapter is generally printed in small capitals, the first letter of the word being a large capital.
3. In handbills and advertisements, all important words are capitalized, so as to attract special attention.

Rule IX. *Titles of Persons.*—All titles of respect or honor should be capitalized.

There are three classes of titles:—

   1. Common Titles.

      Mr., Mrs., Miss, Master.

   2. Professional Titles.

      Prof., Dr., D. D., LL. D., &c.

   3. Official Titles.

      Hon., His Excellency, His Honor, President, Secretary, Senator, Mr. Chairman, &c.

EXAMPLES.

President Hayes, Senator Morton, Hon. Thomas W. Ferry, Dr. Chas. Rynd, Mr. Fred. J. Todd.

REMARKS.

1. A distinction should always be made between words used as titles, and words used in a general sense. For example, senator should commence with a small letter, if it is not placed

before the name of a person as a title, or does not refer to a particular individual. This is the same with president, secretary, doctor, &c.; as, "A patient owes some thanks to a doctor who restores him with nectar smooth and fragrant, instead of rasping his throat and flaying his interior with the bitters sucked by sour-tempered roots from vixenish soils."—*Winthrop.*

2. Father, brother, sister, aunt, uncle, cousin, &c., should commence with a capital, when they are used like titles with the names of persons; as, Father Pierce, Cousin Blackmar.

3. Sir, father, brother, friend, &c., when used as introductory words to a letter, should commence with capitals, as a mark of respect; as, My dear Sir, My dear Friend.

4. In writing such titles as the President of the United States, Secretary of State, Alexander the Great, all the words in the title should commence with a capital, except *of* and *the*.

RULE X. *The Deity.*—All names of the Supreme Being or his Son should commence with a capital.

EXAMPLES.

"But it is now time to depart,—I to die, but you to live. But which of us is going to the better state is unknown to every one but God."—*Socrates.*

"For God so loved the world that he gave his only begotten Son, that whosoever believeth in him should not perish but have everlasting life."—*John iii. 16.*

REMARKS.

1. Writers differ somewhat in the use of capitals in words referring to the Deity. Some capitalize all words in any

way referring to the Supreme Being, while others simply capitalize the words that to them seem important. There should be some uniformity in the use of capitals in words of this character. As a general rule, it is better to follow the usage of an authorized version of the Scriptures.

2. Such words as First Cause, First Principle, Almighty God, Supreme Being, Lord God Almighty, Infinite One, should always be written with capitals.

3. King of kings, Lord of lords, Son of man, Father of lights, Father of spirits, God of hosts, Father of mercies, Prince of life, Prince of kings, and expressions of a similar character, should only commence with a capital. This is the almost invariable usage of the Scriptures. These expressions are not commonly used in the Bible as titles, in the strict sense of the word. For example, King of kings really means that the Deity is the supreme King of all human kings. For illustration see 1 Tim. vi. 15; Dan. vii. 13; Jas. i. 17; Heb. xii. 9; Psa. lxxx. 7; 2 Cor. i. 3; Acts iii. 15; Mat. xii. 32. When these forms are used as titles, they may be capitalized like titles.

4. The adjectives eternal, divine, heavenly, are not printed with capitals in the Scriptures, when referring to the Deity; as, the eternal God, heavenly Father. See Deut. xxxiii. 27; Heb. ix. 14; Mat. vi. 32; 2 Pet. i. 3. When, however, these adjectives are used in an emphatic or special sense, they may commence with capitals.

5. The pronouns referring to the Deity should not be capitalized, when they are used with some name of the Supreme Being; as, "At that time Jesus answered and said, I thank thee, O Father, Lord of heaven and earth, because thou hast hid these things from the wise and prudent, and hast revealed them to babes."—*Mat. xi. 25.* Any chapter of the New Testament will give similar illustrations.

When, however, a pronoun referring to the Deity stands alone, it should commence with a capital; as,—

"O Thou! with whom the night is day,
And one the near and far away."—*Whittier*

6. The capitalization of pronouns is sometimes carried to a ridiculous excess by some writers, especially in poetry; as,

"We praise Thee, O God! for the Son of Thy love."

7. God, goddess, deity, applied to heathen divinities, should not commence with a capital.

RULE XI. *Quotations.*—When the exact words of another are given, the first word of the quotation should commence with a capital, if it forms a complete sentence.

EXAMPLES.

"When the celebrated Chesterfield was asked by a Parisian lady, 'Why, my Lord, does England still retain Christianity?' 'Madame,' he replied, with that mixture of repartee and philosophy which met the case he was dealing with,' Madame, because, as yet, we have been able to find nothing better.'"

Fielding somewhere says, "A good face is a letter of recommendation."

REMARKS.

1. When a quotation is introduced by *that*, it should not commence with a capital; as, Napoleon banished Madame de Stael because he said that " she carried a quiver of arrows that could hit a man if he were seated on a rainbow."

2. When only a part of a sentence is quoted, a small letter should be used; as, "For what satisfaction hath a man,

that he shall 'lie down with kings and emperors in death,' who in his lifetime never greatly coveted the society of such bedfellows?"—*Lamb.*

3. Sometimes a single word comprises the entire saying of another. When this is so, it should commence with a capital; as, "He shouted, 'Victory.'"

4. When examples are given as illustrations of some general principle, they naturally follow the same rule as quotations. If an entire sentence is given as an example, it should commence with a capital. When disconnected words are given, small letters may be used, unless the words themselves require capitals.

RULE XII. *Resolutions.*—In writing resolutions, the word immediately following *Resolved*, should commence with a capital.

EXAMPLE.

"*Resolved*, That the Declaration, passed on the fourth, be fairly engrossed on parchment, with the title and style of 'The Unanimous Declaration of the Thirteen United States of America;' and that the same, when engrossed, be signed by every member of Congress."

REMARK.

Resolved commences with a capital in resolutions, and a comma immediately precedes *That*.

RULE XIII. *Special Words.*—Words used in a special sense, or of special importance, commence with capitals.

EXAMPLES.

"As nowadays we build monuments to great men, so in the Middle Ages they built shrines or chapels on the spots which saints had made holy."—*Froude.*

"The Reformation broke the theological shackles in which men's minds were fettered."—*Froude.*

"That Popularity is alone valuable and enduring which follows you, not that which you run after."—*Lord Mansfield.*

REMARK.

Although it is the universal custom to capitalize a word when used in a special sense to mark an important period or event in history, there is another class of words to which writers assign a special importance, the capitalization of which must necessarily be left to the judgment and taste of each writer. It should, however, be remembered that an injudicious or too frequent use of capitals lessens their value and force, and disfigures a written or printed page.

RULE XIV. *Words Personified.*—When things without life are represented as persons, they may commence with capitals.

EXAMPLE.

"Father Time is not always a hard parent, and though he tarries for none of his children, he often lays his hand lightly upon those who have used him well; making them old men and women inexorably enough, but leaving their hearts and spirits young and in full vigor. With such people the gray head is but the impression of the old fellow's hand in giving them a blessing, and every wrinkle but a notch in the quiet calendar of a well-spent life."—*Dickens.*

REMARK.

Care should be taken **not to** carry this rule **to** an excess. Unless the personification is vivid and emphatic, use small letters; as,—

"Many a daylight dawned and darkened,
Many a night shook off **the** daylight
As the pine shakes off the snow-flakes
From the midnight of its branches."—*Longfellow.*

RULE XV. *I and O.*—The pronoun *I* and the interjection *O* should always **be written with capitals.**

EXAMPLES.

" True faith, I tell thee,
Must ever be the dearest friend **to man:**
His nature prompts him to **assert its** rights."—*Schiller.*

"As wise **as when I went** to school."—*Goeth.*

"O day! O day! O day! O hateful day!
Never was seen **so black a** day as this."—*Shakespeare.*

RULE XVI. *References.*—In referring to passages in books, numbers are sometimes represented by capital letters.

EXAMPLES.

Irving's " Life of Washington," vol. III. p. 77.
Mommsen's " History of Rome," vol. IV. p. 18.

REMARKS.

1. Some commence volume and chapter with a capital, but this is not the usual custom.

2. The volume, chapter, and page may be given, but the volume and page are sufficient.

3. In referring to passages in the Bible, the chapter and verse are given; as Luke, chap. ix. 15. It is the usual custom to omit the word *chapter*, the letters representing the chapter; and the number, the verse; as, "It may be fit to remember that Moses, Lev. xi. 9, Deut. xiv. 9, appointed fish to be the chief diet of the best commonwealth that ever yet was."—*Izaak Walton.*

RULE XVII. *Divisions of a Statement.*—When a general statement is divided into separate and distinct parts, it is better to commence each division with a capital, even when they do not form complete sentences, and are not separated from each other by a period. This is especially the case when the divisions are numbered.

EXAMPLE.

"The history of the normal development of the individual has its counterpart in the history of humanity. There is, 1. The age of popular and unconscious morality; 2. The transitional, skeptical, or sophistical age; and 3. The philosophic or conscious age of morality."

REMARKS.

1. **When** each division commences with a capital and is also numbered, they will be more readily recognized and understood.

2. Some writers number the divisions, but do not commence them with capitals; as, "The teaching of composition requires, (1) a cultivation of thought; and (2) a cultivation of the faculty of expression." It is better to commence each division with a capital.

3. When a sentence is broken off to commence a new line, in order to give special prominence to a statement, or to attract attention, a capital should be used; as,—

    I am, dear Mother,
      Your dutiful son,
        Sam. Johnson.

Letter-Forms.

INTRODUCTION.

In writing letters, or in preparing anything for the press, care should be taken to write a plain, readable hand. Many a valuable position has been lost because of poor penmanship, and many worthy productions have been thrown into the wastebasket, because they have been poorly written. Men of distinction can afford to write a poor hand, to the inconvenience of friends, and the trouble of printers, but, as a general rule, a poor writer labors under a great disadvantage.

The following facts should be remembered in writing letters:—

1. A letter should not be written on half a sheet of paper, unless it is a business letter.

2. Business letters should be as brief as clearness will permit.

3. It is never allowable to write across a written page.

4. All unnecessary flourishes should be avoided.

5. Black ink is preferable, and it is more durable than any other.

THE ADDRESS.

INTRODUCTORY REMARK.

The most important part of letter-writing is to properly direct a letter. During the past year, nearly 4,000,000 letters found their way to the Dead Letter Office, 67,000 of which were misdirected. When we consider the loss to business firms in not promptly receiving important letters, the anxiety to friends and relatives in the delay of expected letters, the expense to the government in sending them to the Dead Letter Office, and in handling and returning them to the writers, the proper direction of a letter becomes a matter of very serious importance.

Definition.—The address consists of the title and name of the person to whom the letter is written, the city and the state in which he lives; as,—

Mr. William K. Bixby,
Houston,
Texas.

REMARKS.

1. Care should be taken to write the address in a clear, bold hand.
2. The usual titles are Mr., Mrs., Miss, and Master. The last title is used in addressing a boy.

3. Esq. is sometimes placed after the name, instead of placing Mr. before. It is used more especially with the names of lawyers, artists, and men of social position. When Esq. is used, never use Mr.

Position.—The title and name should be written about the middle of the envelope, beginning on the left. Below the title and name, and farther to the right, should be written the city; below the city, the state.

REMARKS.

1. It is customary to abbreviate the name of the state. Great care, however, should be taken to properly abbreviate the word. Some abbreviations are so similar to each other that mistakes frequently arise.

2. The address should never be written diagonally.

Punctuation.—A comma should be placed after the name of the person, and after the name of the city. A period should be placed at the end.

REMARKS.

1. Mr., Mrs., Esq., Rev., Dr., Prof., Pres., Capt., &c., are all abbreviations, and consequently the abbreviations should be indicated by a period. Miss is not an abbreviation, and thus requires no mark after it. Messrs. is also an abbreviation. It is used in addressing a firm, but it is frequently omitted.

2. If any part of a person's name is abbreviated, a period should always be used to indicate the abbreviation; as, John S. C. Abbott. The S. and C. without a period really mean nothing.

3. Some place a comma between the parts of a person's name. This, of course, is incorrect. See p. 16 d.

4. All the words in the address should be capitalized, except prepositions and articles.

Honorary Titles.—It is customary to give the professional title or titles of the person to whom a letter is directed, and if he occupies some responsible position, this also should be indicated in the address; as,—

  Rev. E. O. Haven, D.D., LL.D.,
   Chancellor of Syracuse University,
        Syracuse,
          N. Y.

REMARKS.

1. Honorary titles should be given for two reasons:—
   (*a*) As a mark of respect.
   (*b*) The address will be more readily recognized by postmasters, and the letter will be more likely to reach its destination without delay.

2. When titles are written after a person's name, a comma should be placed after each title, for the reason that a comma would be necessary, if the title was written out in full; as, A. M., D.D., LL.D.

3. Some writers make the mistake of placing a period after the first L in LL.D. This title stands for Doctor of Laws, the LL. indicating the plural of Law. As the two letters stand for one word, the period must necessarily be placed after the second L.

4. Hon. applies to judges, senators, representatives, heads of government departments, mayors, and others of similar rank; as, Hon. Thomas M. Cooley.

5. His Excellency applies to the President of the United States, an Ambassador of the United States, or the Governor of a State. This title should be written on a line by itself; as,—

>His Excellency,
>>Gov. C. M. Croswell,
>>>Adrian,
>>>>Mich.

6. In addressing a married lady, the professional title of her husband is sometimes used; as, Mrs. Dr. Haven.

7. Two professional titles meaning the same thing should never be used; as, Dr. A. D. Smith, M. D.

Large Cities.—When the person to whom the letter is addressed, lives in a large city where letters are delivered at places of business or private residences, the title and name, number of house and street, the city, and state should be given; as,—

>A. S. Barnes & Co.,
>>34 and 36 Madison St.,
>>>Chicago.
>>>>Ill.

REMARKS.

1. The title and name should be written first, the number and street to the right and a little below, the city below the name of the street, and the state under the city.

2. The name of the state might be omitted in the address above given. It is not really necessary to give the state, when the city is so widely known that no mistake can arise, if the name of the state is omitted; as, New York, Philadelphia, Boston.

Small Towns and Villages.—The name of the county in which a small town or village is located, should always be given in the address. If the person to whom the letter is written, lives in the country, the nearest post-office must be given, together with the county and state. The name of the place in which a person lives, and his post-office address, may be two very different things.

    Mr. George Harvey,
      Palmyra,
        Lenawee Co.,
          Mich.

REMARKS.

1. The title and name should be written first; the town, village, or post-office, second; the county, third; the state last.

2. Sometimes letters are detained at post-offices, by reason of the directions not being sufficiently complete.

Addressed Envelopes.—It is the custom with business firms, when an answer to a letter is asked as a favor, to send, within the letter, a stamped envelope properly addressed. The address is usually printed, so that no mistake can be made. In all cases, even when an addressed envelope is not required, when a favor is asked from an acquaintance or a friend, and an answer is desired, a postage stamp should always be inclosed. It is certainly an unpardonable presumption to ask even a friend to write a letter for a particular purpose, and expect him to pay for its proper delivery.

Letters with Special Request.—Sometimes directions are written or printed on envelopes as to the disposal of letters, if not called for within a certain time. This should always be done when addressing business letters. These directions are written or printed on the left of the envelope, near the top. See form on p. 81.

The Stamp.—The stamp should be placed in the right-hand corner of the envelope, near the top. It seems hardly necessary to say that every letter should be properly stamped, and yet between three and four hundred thousand letters are annually sent to the Dead Letter Office, because the writers had forgotten to properly stamp them.

FORMS OF ADDRESS.

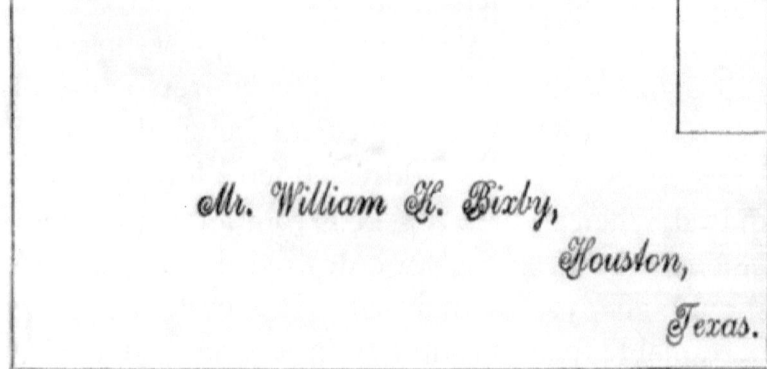

Rev E. O. Haven, D. D., LL. D.,
     Chancellor of University,
          Syracuse,
               N. Y.

Hon. Wm. M. Evarts,
     Secretary of State,
          Washington,
               D. C.

To the President,
     Executive Mansion,
          Washington,
               D. C.

His Excellency,
  Gov. C. M. Croswell,
    Adrian,
      Mich.

Miss Nellie Sedgley,
  215 Prospect Street,
    Cleveland,
      Ohio.

Mr. H. D. Cable,
  Care of A. S. Barnes & Co.,
    34 & 36 Madison St.,
      Chicago.

Miss Venie F. Jones,
Lebanon,
Wilson Co.,
Tenn.

Prof. Moses Coit Tyler, LL. D.
Ann Arbor,
Mich.

Introducing Mr. Abram Stevenson.

If not called for in 10 days, return to
A. S. BARNES & CO.,
34 & 36 Madison Street,
CHICAGO.

Rev. Richard Hudson, A. M.,
Adrian,
Mich.

> *Miss Maude Weaver,*
>
> *City.*
>
> *Kindness of Miss Emma Nash.*

A letter of Introduction should be left unsealed.

> *Miss Florence Bruce,*
>
> *City.*

When a letter is intrusted to an acquaintance or to a friend for delivery, it should not be sealed.

LETTER-FORMS.

I. Adrian, Mich., Nov. 6, 1877.

II. { Mr. William K. Bixby,
       Houston, Texas.

III. Dear Sir,—

IV. Your favor * * *
* * * * * * * *

V. { Very truly,
     Joseph M. Blain.

In the letter-form above given, there are five parts to be considered:—

    I. THE HEADING.
   II. THE ADDRESS.
  III. INTRODUCTORY WORDS.
  IV. THE BODY OF THE LETTER.
   V. THE CONCLUSION.

I. THE HEADING.

Definition.—The heading consists of the name of the city in which the writer lives, the state, the month, the day of the month, and the year; as,—

    Adrian, Mich., Nov. 6, 1877.

REMARKS.

1. Great care should always be taken to give in the heading, not only the city, but also the state. If the letter should be sent to the Dead Letter Office, the heading will properly indicate the place to which the letter is to be returned.

2. The heading indicates to the person who receives the letter where an answer is to be sent.

3. Sometimes the day of the week is given; as, Adrian, Monday, Nov. 5, 1877.

Punctuation.—A comma should be placed after the city, state, and date. A period should be placed at the end. If a word is abbreviated, a period should be used to indicate the abbreviation, and a comma should also be used, if the word written out in full would require a comma; as,—

 Adrian, Michigan, November 6, 1877.
 Adrian, Mich., Nov. 6, 1877.

REMARKS.

1. Some writers thoughtlessly place a comma between the name of the month and the day of the month; as, November, 6, or Nov., 6. The 6 forms an essential part of the month, and should not be separated from it by a punctuation mark.

2. It is better to omit *st*, *th*, or *d* after the number indicating the day of the month. It certainly looks neater to write the date without the marks and dots that sometimes disfigure the heading of letters.

3. Some prefer to place the number before the name of the month; as, Adrian, Mich., 6 Nov., 1877. This, however, is not the usual practice.

Large Cities.—In large cities where letters are delivered by letter-carriers, it is necessary to give, in the heading of a letter, the number of the house and the name of the street. The order should be number, street, city, state, month, day of the month, year; as,—

215 Prospect St., Cleveland, Ohio,
March 5, 1877.

REMARKS.

1. Sometimes the size of the paper necessitates the use of three lines for the heading. If this should be necessary, the number of the house and the name of the street should be on the first line; the city and state, on the second; the month, the day of the month, and year, on the third. Each line should commence farther to the right than the preceding; as,—

215 Prospect St.,
Cleveland, Ohio,
March 5, 1877.

2. As few lines as possible should be used in the heading. In sending letters from well known cities like New York, Philadelphia, &c., it is not necessary to give the state. When the name of the state is omitted, the heading can usually be written on two lines.

3. A period should be placed after St., because it is an abbreviation. A comma should also follow the period, because the word written in full would require a comma. 215 Prospect St., is one item; Cleveland, a second; Ohio, a third; March 5, a fourth; 1877, a fifth.

A Small Town or Village.—If the place in which the writer lives, is a small town or village, the name of the place, county, and state should be given; as,—

Palmyra, Lenawee Co., Mich.,
Sept. 13, 1877.

REMARKS.

1. The county should be given so that an answer to the letter may be properly directed.

2. If the writer lives in the country, the post-office where his letters are received, should be given, and not the place where he lives.

Hotels.—When a letter is written at some prominent hotel, it is customary to give the name of the hotel in the heading; as,—

Grand Central Hotel, New York,
Jan. 10, 1877.

Seminaries and Colleges.—In writing from a seminary, college, or university, the name of the institution is sometimes given; as,—

Female Seminary, Cleveland, Ohio,
April 11, 1877.

Position.—The heading should be written on the first line, on the right hand, commencing about the middle of the line. If more than one line is required, the second line should commence farther to the right than the first, and the third than the second.

REMARKS.

1. When a letter does not fill a full page, the heading should not be written on the first line. The space at the head of the letter should be about the same as at the bottom. In business letters, this is not necessary.

2. Some write the city, state, month, &c., at the close of a letter. This is not however, the usual form.

I. THE ADDRESS.

Definition.—The address in the inside of a letter should be the same as the address on the envelope. It consists of the title and name of the person to whom the letter is written, and the place of his residence; as,—

 Mr. William K. Bixby,
    Houston, Texas.

REMARKS.

There are several reasons why the address should be written within the letter:—

1. Business men usually take an impression or make a copy of all letters written by themselves or their agents. It is a great convenience to have the address within the letter, so that it can be referred to, if necessary, at any time.

2. If the envelope is **accidentally torn off**, or is lost by not being properly sealed, the **letter can** still be forwarded to its destination, if the address is **written within**.

3. It is frequently the habit, on receiving a letter, to destroy the envelope. Sometimes, after the envelope is destroyed, the letter is lost. If there is an inside address, the letter, if found, can be **returned**.

Punctuation.—A comma should be placed after the name of the person and of the city. A period should be placed at the end.

REMARKS.

1. By placing *to* before the address, it will be seen that a period is required at its close, just as a period is required at the end of the address on the envelope; as, To William K. Bixby, Houston, Texas.

2. Some writers place a colon after the name of the state, but the practice is not a correct one. A semicolon should never be used.

Large Cities. When the person to whom the letter is written, lives in a large city, the number and name of the street should be given, as on the outside address; as,—

 A. S. Barnes & Co.,
   34 and 36 Madison St., Chicago.

REMARK.

If three lines are necessary, the title and name should be on the first line, the number and street on the second, the city and state on the third.

Small Towns and Villages.—When the letter is addressed to a small town or village, the county in which the town or village is situated, should be given; as,—

    Mr. George Harvey,
        Palmyra, Lenawee Co., Mich.

REMARK.

The title and name should be on one line; the town or village, county, and state should be on the second.

Letters to Intimate Friends or Relatives.—In writing letters to intimate friends or relatives, the address should be written at the close of the letter, at the left, commencing on the line immediately following the signature. It would be too formal to write the address at the head of the letter, and it would not be in keeping with the introductory words which immediately follow; as,—

      Milburn Wagon Works, Toledo, Ohio,
                  Nov. 2, 1877.
Dear Mother,—
        Your letter   *   *   *

* * * * * * * * *

          Very affectionately,
               Edgar W. Curtis.
Mrs. James E. Curtis,
    Adrian, Mich.

REMARK.

When the heading occupies only one line, it is better to leave a blank line between the heading and the address.

Position.—The address should commence on the left, and should be written on, at least, two lines. The title and name should be on one line; the city and state, on the second, and farther to the right. The address, if possible, should be written on two lines. If the heading consists of two or three lines, the address should commence on the line immediately following the heading. If the heading consists of one line only, a blank line should be left between the heading and the address.

III. INTRODUCTORY WORDS.

Definition.—The introductory words consist of the greeting or salutation; as,—

Dear Sir,—

REMARKS.

1. Sometimes only one word is used in the greeting; as, Sir, Gentlemen.

2. When Sir, Gentlemen, Friend, Father, &c., are used as introductory words, they should always commence with a capital, as a mark of respect. In greeting friends or relatives, do not belittle them with small letters.

3. When dear, respected, honored, and words of a like character, are not the first words of the salutation, they

should commence with a small letter; as, My dear **Sir**, My respected Friend. **If they** commence the salutation, capitals should be **used**; as, **Dear Father,** Respected Friend.

Punctuation.—A comma should be placed after the salutation, and a dash may also be used. The use of the dash, however, is simply a matter of taste.

REMARKS.

1. A colon should not be **placed** after the greeting, except in official or very formal salutations. See p. 100.
2. A semicolon should never be used.

Position.—The introductory words may be written in three different positions:—

1. When the address occupies two lines, the salutation should be written **on the line** immediately following, commencing a little **to the** right of the second line of the address; as,

 Mr. Harry B. Hutchins,
  Mt. Clemens, Mich.
   Dear Sir,—

2. If the address consists of three lines, the first word of the salutation **commences on a line** with the number of the street; as,—

 A. S. Barnes & Co.,
  34 and 36 Madison **St.,**
   Chicago.
 Gentlemen,—

3. If the address is written at the close of the letter, the introductory words should commence on a line with the body of the letter, that is, with the marginal line; as,—

Dear Manning,—

Rest you merry in your own opinion. Opinion is a species of property; and though I am always desirous to share with my friend to a certain extent, I shall ever like to keep some tenets, and some property, properly my own. * * * * *

Your well-wisher and friend,
C. Lamb.

Forms of Salutation.—Custom authorizes the use of several forms of salutation. These may be arranged under four heads:—

1. *To Strangers.*
Sir, Madame, Miss —.

2. *To Acquaintances.*
Dear Sir, Dear Madame, Dear Miss —.
My dear Sir, My dear Madame, My dear Miss —, imply a better acquaintance than Dear Sir, &c.

3. *To Friends or Relatives.*
Dear Friend, My dear Father, Dear Henry, &c.

4. *To Business Firms or Corporate Bodies.*
Sirs, Gentlemen, Ladies.

Salutations to Young Ladies.—Owing to the fact that we have no word corresponding to Sir that can be used in addressing young ladies, there is sometimes an uncertainty as to the proper salutation to be used. Although Madame may refer to a married or an unmarried lady, it is not an appropriate word with which to address a young lady. There are three forms that may be used:—

1. *To a Stranger.*

      Decatur, Ill., May 6, 1877.
Miss Della L. Corbus,—

    * * * * *

      Respectfully,
       William C. Johns.
Miss Della L. Corbus,
  Adrian, Mich.

The name is given as the salutation, and the full address is given at the close of the letter.

2. *To an Acquaintance.*

      Adrian, Mich., Sept. 3, 1877.
Dear Miss Dewey,—

    * * * * * *

      Very truly,
       Thomas M. Hunter.
Miss Ella Dewey,
  Hotel Madison, Toledo, Ohio.

3. *To an Intimate Friend.*—In writing to intimate friends, the character of the letter, and the intimacy of the writers, will suggest the proper forms.

Salutations to Married Ladies.

1. *To a Stranger.*

Mrs. J. C. Hill,
    Adrian, Mich.
        Madame,—

2. *To an Acquaintance.*

Mrs. W. S. Sears,
    Adrian, Mich.
        Dear Madame,—

3. *To a Friend.*

        66 Summit St., Toledo, Ohio,
           Dec. 1, 1877.

Dear Mrs. Millard,—

    *   *   *   *   *   *

        Very truly,
           Franklin Hubbard.

Mrs. A. L. Millard,
    Adrian, Mich.

IV. BODY OF THE LETTER.

The First Word.—The first word should commence on the line immediately following the introductory words, and directly under the comma or the dash of the salutation; as,—

Dear Sir,—
      Your letter   *   *   *   *   *

REMARK.

Some writers commence the body of the letter on the same line with the greeting.

Margin.—It is the usual custom to leave a margin on the left of a written page. This varies according to the taste of the writer and the size of the page.

Paragraphs.—A new paragraph should commence whenever a new subject is introduced, and, with the exception of the first paragraph, which begins directly under the comma or the dash of the salutation, each paragraph should commence a little to the right of the marginal line.

V. THE CONCLUSION.

Definition.—The conclusion is made up of two parts,—words of respect or affection, and the signature of the writer; as,—

      Very truly,
          Joseph M. Blain.

REMARKS.

1. Various forms of respect or affection are used in concluding letters; as, Respectfully, Most respectfully, Very affectionately, &c.

2. In using words of respect or affection, the first word only should be capitalized. In the salutation, Sir, Friend, &c., should commence with a capital, as a mark of respect; but in the conclusion of a letter, it would, to say the least, be in bad taste to give the same prominence to one's own worth.

3. The conclusion should always be in keeping with the introductory words. If Sir were used in the salutation, it would not be proper to use Very affectionately at the close.

4. Although custom sanctions the use of Your obedient servant, Your most obedient servant, and similar forms, the practice is not to be commended. These expressions are associated with a past age, when men depended on the uncertain patronage of the great.

Punctuation.—A comma should be placed after the words of respect and affection, and a period should be placed at the end of the signature.

REMARK.

There is great carelessness exhibited by all writers in punctuating their names. A period should always be placed at the end of the signature, to indicate that the signature is complete. If the different parts of the name are written out in full, no punctuation marks should be placed between them; if, however, any part of the name is abbreviated, a period should always be used to indicate the abbreviation; as, Ettie Shier, Laura B. Palmer, Geo. L. Bennett.

Position.—The conclusion should be written on, at least, two lines. The words of respect and affection should be written on the line immediately following the close of the letter, on the right, commencing near the middle of the line; the signature should be on the line immediately following the words of respect and affection, a little farther to the right.

The Signature.—In signing one's name, there are several important facts to be remembered:—

1. The writer's full name should always be given, especially in business letters and in letters containing money, so that the letter can be returned, if, for any reason, it is sent to the Dead Letter Office. This, of course, can not be done unless the writer's name is given in full. Thousands of dollars are lost every year by writers thoughtlessly signing themselves Nellie, Fred., &c. 25,000 letters, containing $1,301,780, were sent to the Dead Letter Office in the year 1877.

2. A lady, in writing to a stranger, should always sign her name so that the person receiving the letter will know, in answering, whether to address a single or a married lady; as, Miss Maria S. Colvin, Mrs. David Finley.

3. It is frequently the custom for married ladies to use their husband's name; as, Mrs. E. B. Pond. Widow ladies use their Christian name.

4. If the person writing a letter to a stranger, occupies a responsible or official position, he should give this in connection with his signature, so that the person to whom the letter is written, may have some means of knowing how much attention to give to the letter.

SUMMARY.

I. *To a Relative.*

    Ann Arbor, Mich., Nov. 15, 1877.
Dear Father,—
    Your letter   *   *   *   *
*   *   *   *   *   *   *   *   *   *
     Affectionately,
      James A. Stacy.
C. A. Stacy, Esq.,
  Adrian, Mich.

II. *To an Intimate Friend.*

The form of a letter to an intimate friend should be the same as the preceding one.

 Salutation to a married lady, p. 94.

III. *To an Acquaintance.*

    Bay City, Mich., Dec. 4, 1877.
Mr. Wm. B. Mumford,
  Adrian, Mich.
   Dear Sir,—
     Your letter *   *
*   *   *   *   *   *   *   *   *   *
    Very truly,
     William T. Smalley.

1. Salutation to a married lady, p. 94.
2. Letter-form to a young lady, p. 93.

IV. *To a Stranger.*

The same form should be used as to an acquaintance, with the exception of the salutation, which should be Sir, Madame, or Miss—.

Letter-form to a young lady, p. 93.

V. *Letter with Number and Street.*

34 and 36 Madison St., Chicago,
Sept. 12, 1877.

Mr. Charles Scribner,
   124 Grand St., N. Y.
         Dear Sir,—
               Your favor * *
* * * * * * * * * *
               Respectfully,
                  A. S. Barnes & Co.

1. For another form, see p. 91.
2. County and state, pp. 86, 89.
3. Hotels, pp. 86, 93.
4. Seminaries and colleges, p. 86.

VI. *Official Letters.*

150 Summit St., Toledo, Ohio,
Dec. 10, 1877.

Hon. Samuel J. Randall,
   Speaker of the House,
      Washington, D. C.
    Sir:—
        * * * * * * * *
               Very respectfully,
                  Fred. L. Geddes.

To the Common Council of the City of Adrian.
   Gentlemen:—
    *   *   *   *   *   *
                  .   Respectfully,
                        W. S. Wilcox.
 For the use of the colon, see p. 91, Rem. 1.

Proof-Reading.

INTRODUCTION.

Most business men, and all professional men, have occasion, more or less, to have something printed for their own use, or to write something for the public press, so that a correct knowledge of some of the simpler marks used by proof-readers, in making corrections and additions, seems imperative. The advice sometimes given to allow the printer to make all corrections, since he is more likely to know what corrections are necessary, is destructive to a clear presentation of what another has written. The printer may understand better than the writer the mechanical part of his work, but "mind reading" has not yet reached such perfection that the compositor can tell, in all instances, what meaning the writer really wishes to convey, and a misconception on the part of the printer may be the means of changing the sense of a whole paragraph.

In preparing anything for the press, a few facts should be remembered:—

1. It is never allowable to write on both sides of a sheet of paper. Only one side should be used, and each page should be properly numbered.

2. The manuscript should be prepared with great

care. It should be properly punctuated, capitalized, and broken into paragraphs. In fact, the copy placed in the hands of the printer should be in a condition to be exactly reproduced. Some expect the printer to dress up in proper form their half expressed, poorly written, and badly punctuated sentences, and if their hieroglyphics and abbreviations are not deciphered to suit their unreasonable expectations, they rail against incompetent printers and blundering proof-readers.

3. Some writers thoughtlessly leave many points unsettled in the manuscript, so as to see "how they look in print," then fill the proof with numberless corrections and additions, and expect the printer to make such changes as the impulse of the moment has suggested. This is certainly a great injustice to the compositor, who usually receives no remuneration for this additional tax on his time and patience. No half finished manuscript ought to be allowed to go into the printer's hand.

4. Whenever it is really necessary to strike out several words, enough words should be substituted in their places to fill the vacant spaces.

DEFINITIONS.

Copy.—This word really means something to be imitated, and it is used by printers when referring to the manuscript of a writer.

Proof-Sheet.—When the copy is set up in type, an impression in ink is taken for corrections. This is called a proof-sheet. In correcting proof, the first thing to be done is to place the copy in the hands of some one to read aloud, while the proof-reader pays attention principally to omissions, the spelling and capitalization of words, and punctuation. After this, the proof should be carefully examined to detect what are called typographical errors, that is, mistakes in type.

Revise.—After the corrections indicated in the proof are made, another impression is taken. This is called the revise. The revise should be carefully compared with the proof, to see that all corrections are made.

INTRODUCTORY REMARK.

Mistakes in the proof should be called attention to by certain marks which will hereafter be described, and the corrections should be indicated in the margin, on the right or left of the line in which they occur. If mistakes are found near the beginning of the line, the corrections should be placed in the margin on the left, otherwise they should be placed on the right. The numbers in the following statements refer to lines of the specimen proof-sheet on pages 111, 112.

I. *Wrong Letters* and *Punctuation Marks*.— The most common mistakes in a proof-sheet are wrong letters and punctuation marks. When these are noticed, a line should be drawn slopingly, from right to left, through each, and the correct letter or punctuation mark witten in the margin. It is better to repeat the line with the correction in the margin, so as to attract attention to the desired change; as, 2, 4, 8. A sloping line should always be placed between corrections opposite the same line, and the corrections should be placed in the order in which they occur.

REMARKS.

1. The correction in the margin should always be placed to the left of the sloping line; as, 2, 3, 4, 8.

2. The period, **dash**, hyphen, **quotation** marks, apostrophe, and reference marks should be distinguished in the margin, thus:—

⊙　—/　/-/　"/　¨/　,/　*/

For illustrations, see 6, 10.

3. If it is necessary to change a capital letter to a small letter, draw a line through the capital, and either write a

small letter in the margin, or the abbreviation *l. c.*, lower case, which indicates that a common letter is to be used; as, 3.

4. The abbreviation *w. f.*, **wrong font**, indicates that a letter is of improper size.

II. *Wrong Words.*—When an entire word is incorrect, a straight line should be drawn through it, and the proper word written in the margin; as, 5.

REMARK.

When it is necessary to change a word, printed in capitals, to small letters, draw a line through the word, and write *l. c.* in the margin; as, 16. See I., Rem. 3.

III. *Omissions.*—If a letter, punctuation mark, or word is omitted, the omission should be indicated by a caret, and the omitted letter, punctuation mark, or word placed in the margin; as, 3, 6.

REMARKS.

1. When the period, dash, hyphen, quotation marks, or reference marks are omitted, they should be distinguished in the margin as in I., Rem. 2.

2. A sloping line should always be made in the margin, to the right of an omitted letter or punctuation mark; as, 3.

3. If several words or lines are omitted, it is sometimes necessary to write the words at the top or bottom of the proof. When this is the case, a line should be drawn from the caret to the words to be inserted; as, 25.

4. Sometimes so much has been omitted that it is necessary to refer to the copy. When this is so, indicate the omission by a caret, write *See Copy* in the margin, and inclose

within parenthetical marks or brackets the portion of the copy to be inserted in the proof.

IV. *Inverted Letter.*—When a letter is inverted, a sloping line should be drawn through it, and the change indicated in the margin by ꘖ, a character resembling an inverted 6; as, 13.

REMARK.

Some proof-readers draw a line under the inverted letter, but this is not so easily recognized as a sloping line drawn through the letter.

V. *Strike Out.*—It is sometimes necessary to strike out a letter, punctuation mark, or word. A line should be drawn through each, as in I. and II., and the sign ℐ, which means strike out, placed in the margin; as, 9, 19.

VI. *Capitals and Italics.*—Three lines drawn under a word indicate that the word should be printed in large capitals; two lines, small capitals; one line, italics. The abbreviations, *Caps.*, *S. Caps.*, *Ital.*, should also be written in the margin; as, 1, 2.

REMARKS.

1. If a word is italicized, and it is desirable to change it to the ordinary type, draw a line under it, and write *Rom.*, the abbreviation for Roman, in the margin; as, 15.

2. To change a word printed in capitals to small letters, see II., Rem.

VII. *Spacing*.—When there is too great a space between two letters, the letters should be connected by the marks ⌒, and the same sign should be repeated in the margin; as, 21. The single mark ⌣ connecting two words and repeated in the margin, indicates too great a space between words; as, 23.

When there is not sufficient space between two words, a caret is used to indicate the want of space, and the sign # written in the margin; as, 25.

REMARKS.

1. When there is not space enough between two lines, or there is too much, the fact can be indicated as in 7 and 8, 13 and 14.

2. When a space is not left at the commencement of a paragraph, a caret indicates the want of space, and the sign ▭ is placed in the margin; as, 17.

VIII. *Paragraphs*.—When a new paragraph is desired, the sign [should be inserted in the proof, before the first word of the new paragraph, and the sign ¶ should be placed in the margin; as, 10.

When two paragraphs are to be run together, they should be connected by a line, and *No* ¶ written in the margin; as, 24.

REMARKS.

1. The line connecting the two paragraphs is usually so readily recognized that an additional sign in the margin is not always required.

2. For space at the commencement of a paragraph, see VII., Rem. 2.

IX. *Correction to be Disregarded.*—Dots placed under a word, and *Stet.*, which means let it stand, written in the margin, indicate that a correction is to be disregarded; as, 25.

X. *Broken Letters.*—When it is necessary to call the attention of the printer to a broken letter, a line should be drawn under it, and the sign × placed in the margin; as, 21.

REMARK.

It is the custom with some proof-readers to draw a sloping line through the broken letter, and repeat the letter in the margin. This is sometimes a great convenience to the printer, especially when the letter is so badly injured that it can not be recognized; for, unless the printer is familiar with the spelling of the word, it may be necessary, with considerable inconvenience, to refer to the copy.

XI. *Transpose.*—When two words should change places, the custom is to draw a line over the first, continue it under the second, and write *tr.*, the abbreviation for transpose, in the margin; as, 26.

REMARKS.

1. When several letters in a word are not in their proper order, either draw a line through the word and rewrite it in the margin, or draw a line under or through the letters, and write them in their proper order.

2. When the order of several words is to be changed, indicate the proper order by placing 1, 2, 3, 4, &c., over the words, draw a straight line under each, and write *tr.* in the margin.

XII. *Crooked Words.*—When the letters of a word are displaced, draw a line above and below the word, and repeat the lines in the margin; as, 28. The same marks are used to call attention to a crooked line.

XIII. *Projecting Leads.*—When a lead projects so as to leave an impression on the proof, a sloping line should be drawn through it, and the sign ⊥ or ⊥ placed in the margin; as, 22.

XIV. *Diphthongs.*—When æ and œ should be printed as diphthongs, a line should be drawn through them, and the letters forming the diphthong written in the margin thus, æ͡, œ͡.

XV. *Mark of Attention.*—The sign + is sometimes used to call the attention of the printer to some defect in a word or line.

GENERAL REMARK.

It is the custom with many proof-readers to draw a line from the mistake in the proof to the correction in the margin. This should always be done when the mistakes are numerous, or the lines crowded together.

Description of a Palace in a Valley.

Ye who listen with credulety to the whispers of Fancy and pursue with egerness the phantoms of hope, who will expect that age shall perform the promises of youth, and that the deficiencies of the present day will be supplyed by the morrow, attend to the history of Rasselass, prince of Abyssinia. [Rasselas was the fourth son of the mighty emperor, in whose dominions the father of waters begins his course; whose bounty pours down the streams of plenty, and scatters over *half* the world the harvest of Egypt.

The place which the wisdom or policy of antiquity had destined for the the residence of the abyssinian princes, was a spacious valley in the kingdom of Amhara, surrounded on every side by mountains, of which the summits overhung the middle part. The only passage by which it could be entered, was a cavern that passed under a rock of which it has been long disputed whether it was the work of nature or of human industry.

Dr. Johnson.

DESCRIPTION OF A PALACE IN A VALLEY.

——o——

Ye who listen with credulity to the whispers of fancy, and pursue with eagerness the phantoms of hope; who expect that age will perform the promises of youth, and that the deficiencies of the present day will be supplied by the morrow, attend to the history of Rasselas, prince of Abyssinia.

Rasselas was the fourth son of the mighty emperor, in whose dominions the father of waters begins his course; whose bounty pours down the streams of plenty, and scatters over half the world the harvests of Egypt.

The place which the wisdom or policy of antiquity had destined for the residence of the Abyssinian princes, was a spacious valley in the kingdom of Amhara, surrounded on every side by mountains, of which the summits overhung the middle part. The only passage by which it could be entered, was a cavern that passed under a rock, of which it has long been disputed whether it was the work of nature or of human industry.

Dr. Johnson.

INDEX.

The first number of each reference refers to the page.

Abbreviations, how indicated, 29, II.; list of, 29, 30; additional marks, 30, 1; proper names, 30, 2; numerals, 30, 3; numbering pages, 30, 4; letter doubled to indicate the plural, 30, 5; how to abbreviate words, 30, 6; Mr., Mrs., etc., 74, 1, 2.

Addressed, person or thing, 13, VIII.; strong emotion, 14 Rem.; 33, III.

Address of envelopes, most important part of letter-writing, 73; position, 74; punctuation, 74; honorary titles, 75; large cities, 76; small towns and villages, 77; addressed envelopes, 77; letters with special request, 78; stamp, 78; forms of address, 78–82.

Address, inside, definition of, 87; punctuation of, 88; large cities, 88; small towns and villages, 89; intimate friends and relatives, 89; position, 90.

Adjectives, two, 17, 2; in a series, 18, 1.

Adverbs, 10, 3.

Advertisements, capitalization of, 62, 3.

Almighty God, 64, 2.

And, or, nor, connecting words in a series, 17, XIV.; words and phrases, 19, 3; phrases and clauses, 18, XV.; 19, 2; *or* between two words or expressions, the latter explaining the former, 18, 2.

Answer and question in the same paragraph, 36, 3.

Apostrophe, the, 47, 48; form of, 47, Rem; denotes what, 47, II See Possession.

Appositives, 15, XI.; definition of, 16, 1; two nouns in appo-

sition, 16, 2, a; noun and pronoun, 16, 2, b; two pronouns, 16, 2, c; parts of a person's name, 16, 2, d.
Arabic numbers, 22, XVIII.
As, 21, 3; introducing an example, 24, Rem.; *as* with a dash, 36, 4.
As it were, 9, IV.; as follows, 27, III.
Aunt, when to commence with a capital, 63, 2, 3; 90, 2; 96, 2.
Author from whom a quotation is taken, 36, 2· manuscript of, 72, 102, 103; correction of proof, 102.

B

Because, 7, 1.
Being or having been, 14, Rem.
Bible, references to. See References.
Body of the letter, the first word, 94; margin, 95; paragraphs, 95.
Books, titles of, 44, II.; chapter, 62, 2; title-pages, 62, VIII.
Brackets, 41, 42; additional marks, 41, 1; reporting speeches, 41, 2; parenthetical marks, 42, 3.
Broken letters in proof, 109, X.
Broken sentences, 34, I.
Brother, when to commence with a capital, 63, 2, 3; 90, 2; 96, 2.
But, 6, 1.

C

Capitals, 54–70; usage formerly, 55; tendency at the present day, 56; value of capitals, 56; how indicated in writing, 53, V.; in proof, 107, VI.; title-pages, 62, VIII.
Caret, 52, II.; in proof, 106, III.
Chapter, first word of, 62, 2.
Church, when written with a capital, 60, 3.
Clauses, definition of, 5; independent, 6, I.; dependent, 6, II.; relative, 7, 8, 9; participial, 14, IX.; series of, 24, III.; concluding, 34, II.; short, 24, Rem. See Expressions.

Colon, the, 25-28; indicates what, 3, 4; not used as much as formerly, 28.
Comma, the, 5-22; indicates a close relationship, 3, 4; omitted, 3; 16, 2; 21, 1, 2, 3; preferred sometimes to semicolons, 25.
Commas, two, placed under a word, 52, I.
Complete sentences, 29, I.; title of essay, oration, etc., 29, Rem.
Compound words, 49, I.; definition of, 49, 1.
Concluding clause, 34, II.; emphatic conclusion, 35, 1; *namely, that is*, etc., omitted, 35, 2; word or expression repeated, 35, 3.
Conclusion of a letter, definition, 95; punctuation, 96; position, 97, signature, 97.
Conclusion, emphatic, 35, I.
Contrasted expressions or comparisons, 20, XVII.; comparison, short, 21, 1.; *so-that, rather-than*, etc., 21, 2; *as, than*, 21, 3; first expression negative, the other affirmative, 21, 4.
Consequently, 9, IV.
Copy, definition of, 104.
Correction in proof to be disregarded, 109, IX.
Cousin, when to commence with a capital, 63, 2, 3; 90, 2; 96, 2.
Crooked words in proof, 110, XII.

D

Dagger, double dagger, uses of, 53, VI.
Dash, 34-38; additional punctuation marks, 38, 1, 2.
Days of the month, 60, VI.; spring, summer, etc., 61, Rem.
Dates, 22, Rem.
Deity, the, 63, X.; difference among writers, 63, 1; First Cause, etc., 64, 2; King of kings, etc., 64, 3; eternal, divine, etc., 64, 4; pronouns, 64, 5; 65, 6; god, goddess, deity, 65, 7.
Democrat, 60, V.

Dependent clauses, 6, II.; definition of, 7, 1; omission of comma, 7, 2.
Devil, 59, 3.
Diaeresis, 50, 4.
Diphthongs, how indicated in proof, 110, XIV.
Direct question, 31, I.
Direct quotation. See **Quotation**.
Divine, 64, 4.
Division of words, 50, III.; where to divide a word, 51, 1.
Divisions of sentences, 23, I.; 25, Gen. Rem.
Divisions of a statement, 69, XVII.; how readily recognized, 70, 1; usage of some writers, 70, 2; sentences broken off to attract attention, 70, 3.

E

East, when to commence with a capital, 59, 1.
Ellipsis, marks of, 52, III.
Emotion, strong, 32, I.; unusual degree, 32, Rem.
Emphasis, words repeated for, 17, 3; use of the dash to give prominence, 37, Gen. Rem.; 35, 1.
Enumeration of particulars, 27, III.; particulars preceded by a colon, 27, 1; not introduced by *thus, following*, etc., 27, 2; particulars preceded by a semicolon, 27, 3; comma and dash sometimes used, 28, 4.
Envelopes, addressed, 77; with special request, 78; with stamp, 78.
Esq., 74, 3.
Eternal, referring to the Deity, 64, 4.
Example, punctuation of words preceding, 24, Rem.; first word of, 66, 4.
Exclamation point, 32, 33; inclosed within parenthetical marks, 40, 3.
Expressions, inverted, 12, VI.; two brief, 19, 2; contrasted,

20, XVII.; complete in themselves, 23, II.; 28, Gen. Rem.; series of, 24, III.; negative and affirmative, 21, 4; at the end of sentences, 22, XIX.; equivalent to sentences, 57, 2.

F

Father, when to commence with a capital, 63, 2, 3.
Federalist, 60, V.
Figures omitted, 36, IV.; Arabic, 22, XVIII.
Finally, 9, IV.
First Cause, First Principle, 64, 2; Father of mercies, Father of spirits, 64, 3.
First word in a sentence, 57, I.; in expressions numbered, 69, XVII.; after a period, 57, 3.
Following, 27, III., 2.
Foreign words, 43, 2.
Forms of address, 78–82.
Friend, when to commence with a capital, 63, 3; 90, 2; 96, 2.

G

General remarks, 28, 37, 110.
God, 63, 64; goddess, 65, 7; God of hosts, 64, 3.
Gospel, 61, 3.
Greeting. See Introductory words.

H

Handbills, use of capitals in, 62, 3.
Heading of letters, 83; definition, 83; punctuation, 84; large cities, 85; a small town or village, 86; hotels, 86; seminaries or colleges, 86; position, 86.
Heaven and hell, 59, 3.
Heavenly, applied to the Deity, 64, 4.
Hers, 48, 3.
Hesitation, how indicated, 34, I.
His, Him, referring to the Deity, 64, 5.

His Excellency, 76, 5; 62, IX.; address of envelope, 80.
Hon., 75, 4; 62, IX.
However, 9, IV.
Hyphen, the, 49–51; connecting several words, 49, 2; omitted, 49, 3; doubt as to the use, 49, 5.

I

I, 68, XV.
If, 7, 1.
Indeed, 9, IV.
Independent clauses, 6, I.; definition of, 6, 1; comma omitted, 6, 2; separation by a semicolon, 6, 3.
Infinite One, 64, 2.
In short, in fact, in reality, 9, IV.
Interjections, 32, II.; exclamation point at the end of a sentence, 33, 1, 2.
Interrogation point, 31, I.; inclosed in parenthetical marks, 40, 2.
Introductory words of letters, definition, 90; punctuation, 91; position, 91; forms of salutation, 92; salutations to young ladies, 93; to married ladies, 94.
Introductory remarks, 5, 73.
Inverted expressions, 12, VI.; explanation, 12, 1; omission of comma, 12, 2.
Inverted letter in proof, 107, IV.
Italics, how indicated, 53, V.; 107, VI.; words from a foreign language, 43, 2; written with or without a capital, 60, Rem.
Its, 48, 3.

K

King of kings, 64, 3.

L

Leaders, 53, IV.

Letters or figures omitted, 36, IV; 3-9 equivalent to, 37, Rem
Letters omitted, 47, I.; the apostrophe, 47, Rem.
Letters, care in writing, some facts, 73.
Letter-forms, 71-100.
List of abbreviations, 29, 30; 30, 7.
LL D., 30, 5; 75, 3.
Logical subject, 19, XVI.; definition of, 20, 1; custom of some writers, 20, 2.
Long sentences, 25, I.
Lord of lords, 64, 3.

M

Madame, 93, 94.
Marks of parenthesis, 39, 40; additional marks, 39, 1; dashes, 37, V.; comma, 40, 4.
Mark of attention in proof, 110, XV.
Members of sentences, 25, Gen. Rem.
Miscellaneous marks, 52, 53.
Miss, 74, 1; 93.
Months and days, names of, 60, VI.; autumn, spring, etc., 61, Rem
More—than, 21, 2.
Moreover, 9, IV.

N

Name, person's, 16, 2, d.; abbreviated, 30, 2; 74, 2; 96, Rem. period used after name, 29, Rem. See Signature.
Namely, 9, IV.; 35, 2.
Nations, names of, 59, IV.; Italics and Italicized, 60, Rem.
Negative expressions, 21, 4.
Nevertheless, 9, IV.
Nor, 6, 1.
Not, contrasted expressions 21, 4.

North, when to commence with a capital, 59, 1.
Nouns in apposition, 15, 16. See Words.
Numeral figures, 22, XVIII.; dates, 22, Rem.

O

O, 68, XV.; not followed by an exclamation point, 32, II.
Of which, 9, 3; of course, 9, IV.
Omitted, letters or figures, 36, IV.; 47, I.
Omissions, how indicated, 52, II.; in proof, 106, III.
Or, 6, 1; 18, 2.
Ours, 48, 3.

P

Pages, numbering of, 30, 4.
Paragraphs, quoted, 46, IV.; sign of, 53, VI.; in proof, 108, VIII.
Parallel lines, 53, VI.
Parenthesis, 39, I.; additional marks, 39, 1, a, b, c; comma and dash often preferred, 37, V.; 40, 4; doubtful assertion, 40, 2; irony or contempt, 40, 3.
Parenthetical words and phrases, 9, IV.; definition of, 10, 1; when commas are omitted, 10, 2; parenthetical words and adverbs, 10, 3.
Parenthetical expressions, 11, V.; distinction between parenthetical expressions and parenthetical words, 11, 1, a, b; when commas are omitted, 11, 2.
Parties, names of, 60, V. See Sects.
Participal clauses, 14, IX.; sign of, 14, Rem
Perhaps, 9, IV.
Period, indicates what, 3; uses of, 29, 30.
Persons and places, names of, 58, III.; North, South, etc., 59, 1; words derived from names of persons, 59, 2; Satan, devil, 59, 3.

Person or thing addressed, 13, VIII.; strong emotion, 14, Rem.

Personification, 67, XIV.

Phrases and clauses, 18, XV.; definition of a phrase, 19, 1; of a clause, 5; when commas are omitted, 19, 2; words and phrases in a series, 19, 3; parenthetical phrases, 9, 10.

Poetry, first word of each line, 58, II.

Political parties, 60, V.

Possession, 47, II.; singular of nouns, 47, 1; plural of nouns, 48, 2; ours, yours, etc., 48, 3.

Prefixes, 50, II.; definition of, 50, 1; vowel and consonant 50, 2; vice-president, etc., 50, 3; when to use the diaeresis, 50, 4.

Prince of life, **Prince of kings**, 64, 3.

Projecting leads in proof, 110, XIII.

Pronouns referring to the Deity, 64, 5; 65, 6.

Proof-reading, 101–114; its importance, 102; preparation of manuscript, 102, 103; copy, proof-sheet, revise, 104; wrong letters and punctuation marks, 105, I.; wrong words, 106, II.; omissions, 106, III.; inverted letter, 107, IV.; strike out, 107, V.; capitals and italics, 107, VI.; spacing, 108, VII.; paragraphs, 108, VIII.; correction to be disregarded, 109, IX.; broken letters, 109, X.; transpose, 109, XI.; crooked words, 110, XII.; projecting leads, 110, XIII.; diphthongs, 110, XIV.; mark of attention, 110, XV.; Gen. Rem., 110.

Proof-sheet, definition of, 104; specimen proof, 111, 112; corrected proof, 113, 114.

Punctuation, its importance, iii., iv.; how to teach it, iv.; V.; principal punctuation marks, 3; other marks, 4; punctuation marks, why used, 3, 4.

Q

Question, direct, 31, I.; question and answer in the same paragraph, 36, 3.

Quotation, short, 12, VII.; long, 13, 5; 26, II.; 27, 1; expressions resembling a quotation, 13, 1; introduced by *that*, 13, 2; 65, 1; single words quoted, 13, 3; 65, 2; 66, 3; quotation divided, 13, 4; quotation in the middle of a sentence, 27, 2; quotation within a quotation, 45, 1; 46, 2; parts of a quotation omitted, 46, IV., 2; first word of a quotation, 65, XI.; examples as illustrations, 24, Rem.; 66, 4.

Quotation marks, 43-46; direct quotation, 43, I.; exact words not given, 43, 1; words from a foreign language, 43, 2; quotation followed by a comma, semicolon, colon, period, 44, 4; by an exclamation or interrogation point, 44, 5, 6; titles of books, 44, II.; quotation within a quotation, 45, III.; paragraphs, 46, IV.

Quoted passage, 41, I.

R

Republican, Radical, 60, V.
Rather—than, 21, 2.
Reference marks, 53, VI.
References, 68, XVI.; volume and chapter, 69, 1; to the Bible, 69, 3; volume and page sufficient, 69, 2.
Relative clauses, 7, III.; commas when used, 7, III., 1; when omitted, 7, III., 2; introduced by *who*, etc., 8, 1; exceptions, 8, 2, 3.
Reporter, remarks by, 41, 2.
Resolutions, 66, XII.; *Resolved* and *That*, 66, Rem.
Revise, definition of, 104.

S

Salutations. See Introductory words.
Scriptures, sacred writings, 61, 3.
Sects, names of, 60, V.; Republican, etc., 60, 1, 2; Church, 60, 3.
Section mark, 53, VI.

Semicolon, 23-25; indicates distant relationship, 3, 4; often preferred to a colon, 28; semicolon and comma, 25.

Sentence, definition of, 5; 57, 1; long sentences, 23, I.; members of, 23, II.; 25, Gen. Rem.; 28, Gen. Rem.; complete sentences, 29, I.; broken sentences, 34, I.; first word of, 57, I.; expressions equivalent to a sentence, 57, 2; word following a period, 57, 3; word following an interrogation or an exclamation, 58, 4.

Series of words, 17, XIV.; commas, when not used, 17, XIV., 1; when used, 18, XIV., 2, 3; last word preceding a single word, 18, 1; two words connected by *or*, 18, 2; series of phrases and clauses, 18, XV.; of expressions, 24, III.

Short quotations. See Quotations.

Signatures, 29, Rem.; 97, 98.

Since, 7, 1.

Sister, when to commence with a capital, 63, 2; 90, 2; 96, 2.

Sir, 63, 3.

Son of man, 64, 3.

So—that, so—as, 21, 2.

South, 59, 1.

Spacing in proof, 108, VII.

Specimen proof, 111, 112.

Special words, capitilization of, 66, 67.

Spring, summer, 61, Rem.

Stamp, 78.

Star, reference mark, 53, VI.

Strike out in proof, 107, V.

Strong emotion, 32, I.; unusual emotion, 32, Rem.

Subject, logical, 19, XVI.; definition of, 20, 1; subject of statement or quotation, 35, III.; definition of, 36, 1; author, 36, 2; question and answer, 36, 3; *as*, *thus*, etc., 36, 4.

Summary of letter-forms, 98-100.

Supreme Being, 64, 2; Son of man, 64, 3.

T

Titles, annexed, 16, 3; of essays, orations, etc., 29, Rem.; 61, 2; of books, 44, II.; 61, VII.; of magazines, 45, 1, 2; of persons, 62, IX.; sacred writings, 61, 3.

Title-pages, 62, VIII.; first word of a chapter, 62, 2; hand-bills and advertisements, 62, 3.

Than, 21, 3.

That, 8, 1; 13, 2; quotation introduced by *that*, 65, 1; in resolutions, 66, Rem.

That is, 35, 2.

Theirs, 48, 3.

Therefore, 9, IV.

Thus, this, these, 27, III.; 27, 2; 36, 4.

To-day, to-night, to-morrow, 49, 4.

Too, 10, 3.

Transpose in proof, 109, XI.

U

Until, 7, 1.

Unconnected words, 16, XIII., comma, when used, 17, 1, 3; when not used, 17, 2.

Uncle, when to commence with a capital, 63, 2, 3; 90, 2; 96, 2.

V

Verb omitted, 15, X.; main clauses separated by a semicolon, 15, 1; comma omitted, 15, 2.

Vice-president, 50, 3.

W

What, 8, 1.

When, 7, 1.

Words, parenthetical, 9, **IV.**; in apposition, 15, XI.; unconnected, 16, **XIII.**; series of, 17, **XIV.**; repeated for emphasis, 17, 3; 35, 3; two connected by *or*, 18, 2; words and phrases in a series, 19, 3; from a foreign language, 43, 2; compound, 49, **I.**; division of, 50, III ; repeated, 52, **I.**; special, 66, **XIII.**

Words personified, 67, **XIV.**; caution, 68, Rem.

Wrong letters and punctuation marks in proof, 105, **I.**; wrong words, 106, **II.**

Y

Yours, 48, 3.

www.ingramcontent.com/pod-product-compliance
Lightning Source LLC
Chambersburg PA
CBHW022134160426
43197CB00009B/1276